Nonprofit Management Simplified

Internal Operations

Marilyn L. Donnellan, MS

D1224404

Nonprofit Management Simplified: Internal Operations

One of the **Nonprofit Management Simplified**™ series

Published by
CharityChannel Press, an imprint of CharityChannel LLC
424 Church Street, Suite 2000
Nashville, TN 37219 USA

CharityChannel.com

Nonprofit Management Simplified, the Nonprofit Management Simplified logo, and book design are trademarks of CharityChannel Press, an imprint of CharityChannel LLC.

ISBN Print Book: 978-1-938077-82-1

Library of Congress Control Number: 2016943356

13 12 11 10 9 8 7 6 5 4 3 2 1

Printed in the United States of America

This and most CharityChannel Press books are available at special quantity discounts for bulk purchases for sales promotions, premiums, fundraising, or educational use. For information, contact CharityChannel Press, 424 Church Street, Suite 2000, Nashville, TN 37219 USA. +1 949-589-5938.

Publisher's Acknowledgments

This book was produced by a team dedicated to excellence; please send your feedback to Editors@CharityChannel.com.

We first wish to acknowledge the tens of thousands of peers who call CharityChannel their online professional home. Your enthusiastic support for the **Nonprofit Management Simplified** series is the wind in our sails.

Members of the team who produced this book include:

Editors

Acquisitions: Linda Lysakowski

Comprehensive Editing: Linda Lysakowski

Copy Editing: Jill McLain

Production

Layout: Joy Metcalf

Illustrations: Kim O'Reilly

Design: Stephen Nill

Administrative

CharityChannel LLC: Stephen Nill, CEO

Marketing and Public Relations: John Millen

About the Author

Marilyn L. Donnellan, MS, fortuitously fell into nonprofit management when the editor of the newspaper where she was working as a reporter suggested she apply for the executive director position of a small nonprofit. Over the next twenty-plus years, she enthusiastically served in five nonprofits, ranging in size from that single staff organization with a $150,000 budget to one with three hundred staff and a $6 million budget. She figured it out along the way, collecting tons of resources to help her with the myriad of responsibilities and challenges.

When her stack of resources got too large to fit in a filing cabinet, Donnellan decided to open a consulting firm to share what she had learned with other nonprofit staff and volunteers. She has been a consultant for more than ten years, helping hundreds of nonprofits build their capacity—although her filing cabinet is still bursting at the seams.

Donnellan is the author of three books on nonprofit management: *Core Elements of a Successful Nonprofit, The Hour Series of Guides for Nonprofit Management* (both published by Nonprofit Management Services LLC), and *The Complete Guide to Church Management* (Xulon Press). She has authored articles in *The Nonprofit Times* and *The Nonprofit Digest*. Her award-winning helps for nonprofits are in use around the world.

Dedication

To Steve, the love of my life, who believes I can do anything and is always there for support, even if it means him sacrificing a round of golf.

Author's Acknowledgments

I could never in a million years have imagined that this poor farm girl from Oregon would one day be a published author. Special thanks go to the board members, staff, and volunteers at all the nonprofits where I served. They patiently taught me so much about what it means to be an excellent manager and how to balance passion with expertise.

Thank you, fellow consultants and clients who encouraged me to keep on writing and who shared so much of your own experiences so I could do my job better.

Thank you, Scott Bechtler-Levin, formerly at IdeaEncore/4Good. You encouraged me to try new methods of marketing. The dozens of consultants and executive directors who reviewed the manuscripts, in spite of their busy schedules, deserve special thanks and kudos. And deep appreciation to everyone at CharityChannel Press, led by the able Stephen Nill, who enthusiastically encouraged my creativity.

Contents

Summary of Chapters

Balancing Competing Demands. Based on the Circle of Management Excellence, strategies and tools are overviewed that will help the manager excel, even with limited resources. Balancing the core elements of a successful nonprofit, and management strategies based on consistent internal controls, will enhance staff and volunteer development and will help the manager be better able to have the time to cultivate potential donors and volunteers.

Foreword

Since my early days in the nonprofit sector, I have been a huge fan of Marilyn Donnellan's work, so I was absolutely thrilled when she asked me to read and review her new book, *Nonprofit Management Simplified: Internal Operations*. Described to me as a compilation of her best training tools (all of which I had already devoured), I couldn't wait to jump into it.

Marilyn notes in her book that at last count, there were more than 1.7 million nonprofits in the United States contributing more than an estimated $1.7 trillion to the economy annually. But it is estimated that 50 percent of start-up nonprofits will close their doors within the first two years.

In her words, "Because the dissolution of a nonprofit is rarely due to the founder lacking passion or good intentions, why do so many folks have problems getting their nonprofits off the ground? Are there some things that can be done to increase the chances of success? Every day, thousands of nonprofits struggle to survive, and sadly, many of them will either fail or limp along for years with their effectiveness limited because their founders failed to take the basic steps essential to providing solid foundations for their nonprofits."

We see it time and time again; nonprofits are so busy and eager to provide programs that they ignore critical infrastructure issues such as board recruitment, financial management, risk management, and marketing. This inefficiency at a management level causes these organizations to struggle to achieve their mission, and they will constantly be looking for funding and wondering why they cannot get or keep good board members and other volunteers.

Nonprofit Management Simplified: Internal Operations was written to help nonprofit executive directors build that solid foundation of excellence by breaking down the core elements of nonprofit management success and providing proven and workable strategies. Helpful field-tested policies, templates, checklists, and procedures are also included for every topic.

If you feel, as the CEO of your organization, that you are always caught up in a flurry of activities, fundraisers, pressing personnel issues, problems with the board, lack of training and programs, and that you don't have time to plan, this book is for you. The three books in this series do not examine the philosophical or theoretical issues of nonprofit management but focus on the proven strategies that have worked again and again for Marilyn as an executive director herself and for the hundreds of organizations she has consulted with over the past thirty years.

Although there is no magic pill that makes someone an excellent executive director, *Nonprofit Management Simplified: Internal Operations* has everything you need to get your organization built on a foundation of excellence and ultimately, dramatically increasing your chances of long-term success and sustainability.

Natasha Golinsky, Founder
Next Level Nonprofits

Introduction

I am convinced that an executive director starting a career as the only staff person in a very small nonprofit has a distinct advantage over an executive director of a large organization.

Why? Because when you are the only staff person, you are forced to learn everything there is to know about everything. When I finally had staff to help with the myriad of responsibilities, my experiences at the small nonprofit greatly enhanced my staff management capabilities. I knew exactly what their job entailed because I had done it myself in the smaller nonprofit.

You do not have the time or the energy to spend weeks or months learning an accounting system or putting together a sophisticated fundraising plan. Every day, you are forced to balance and prioritize all the core elements that make for a successful nonprofit.

I remember early in my nonprofit career thinking maybe I should take a class on marketing. But the reality was I did not have any spare hours to take the class. So I burned the midnight oil reading, attended a periodic workshop, and then just figured it out on my own, striving to break down all the management responsibilities into their simplest and most workable strategies.

The three handbooks in this series do not examine the philosophical or theoretical issues of nonprofit management. Instead, the information simplifies nonprofit management by breaking it down into the core elements, providing proven and workable strategies. Field-tested policies, templates, checklists, and procedures are included for every topic.

This book focuses on all things administrative: starting a nonprofit, finance, personnel management, risk management, assessments, and plain old-fashioned time management.

Nonprofit Management Simplified: Board and Volunteer Development includes everything you need to know about board roles and responsibilities, strategic planning, executive director performance reviews, and the recruitment, training, recognition, and dismissal of all three types of volunteers: board, committee, and program. Also included are hints for effective meetings.

Nonprofit Management Simplified: Programs and Fundraising outlines tools and strategies for developing and assessing the programs from an outcomes measurements approach. Community involvement, marketing, and all types of resource development strategies are examined, with assessment strategies for each element included.

Chapter One

Starting a Nonprofit

IN THIS CHAPTER

- ┅➜ Rationale for a start-up plan
- ┅➜ Board and infrastructure issues
- ┅➜ Funding issues
- ┅➜ Questions to answer
- ┅➜ Developing a business plan
- ┅➜ Legal requirements for starting a nonprofit

Dan Quayle, the forty-fourth vice president of the United States of America, said, "If we don't succeed, we run the risk of failure." While you are scratching your head over those words of wisdom, consider this: It is estimated that 50 percent of start-up nonprofits will close their doors within the first two years.

Why do so many folks have problems getting their nonprofits off the ground? Are there some things that can be done to increase the chances of success? Thousands of nonprofits struggle to survive. And the dissolution of a nonprofit is rarely because the founder's passion or good intentions are lacking.

Sadly, many of them will either fail or limp along for years with their effectiveness limited because their founders failed to take the basic steps essential to providing solid foundations for their nonprofits.

At last count, there were more than 1.7 million nonprofits in the United States, contributing more than an estimated $1.7 trillion into the economy annually. But not all the nonprofits that file for the Internal Revenue Service's 501(c)(3) designation as tax-deductible, tax-exempt charities will succeed.

And in countries like India, where nongovernmental organizations already number more than five million in just a few years, what can they learn from their American counterparts to ensure their success?

Steps for Starting a Nonprofit

If you are thinking about starting a nonprofit or are struggling to keep a nonprofit going, take a look at these key steps for starting a nonprofit. Put your responses to these steps in writing. You really do not have a plan if it is not written down.

Conduct Research about the Competition

Many times, the nonprofit start-up volunteers are commendably passionate about their cause but fail to find out whether or not there are other nonprofits in the area providing the same or similar services, creating unnecessary competition for limited funds. In fact, the number-one problem identified in most community needs and resource assessments is not the lack of resources but the lack of knowing where the resources are. It is better to never start the nonprofit than to start and fail!

> ### Steps for Starting a Nonprofit
>
> ◆ Conduct research about the competition.
>
> ◆ Recruit board members and establish infrastructure.
>
> ◆ Develop a variety of funding methods.
>
> ◆ Train the board and staff on their roles and responsibilities.
>
> ◆ Develop a written business plan.
>
> ◆ Answer basic questions.
>
> ◆ Submit legal documents to all governmental agencies.

I was talking to a food bank client in one of the communities where I served. "Are you getting the help you need?" I asked. "Oh sure," he cheerfully said. "After I pick up my food here, I just go down the street to the other food bank and get more."

Such duplication of effort not only builds dependency in the clients, but it can also stretch limited resources to the breaking point. Even if your nonprofit has been around for a while, do not ignore the

Organizational Structure Based on the Core Elements

need to frequently take a look at what is happening within your community, especially within your specific field of service.

Who is your competition? Can some other nonprofit more effectively provide the services and programs you are struggling to provide? Which is more important: your ego or providing essential services in the most efficient way possible? Are you spending all your time fundraising and running programs? Or have you learned how to balance the time you spend on each of the core management elements to increase the potential for success?

Recruit Board Members and Establish Infrastructure

Although US laws do not require that the start-up nonprofit have more than one board member in order to file for tax exemption, I strongly recommend that you have at least three board members before filing in order to indicate community support for the effort. Set a goal to have a minimum of eleven and a maximum of twenty-five board members within the first two to three years.

Decide what the organizational structure will look like. Both start-up and longtime nonprofits are sometimes so busy and eager to provide programs that they ignore critical infrastructure issues such as

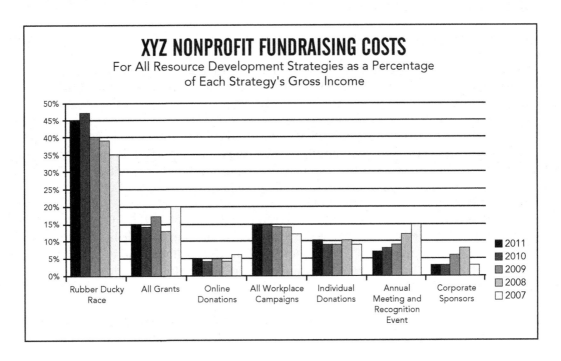

board recruitment, financial management, risk management, and marketing. Even if your nonprofit has been around a while, it is essential to at least annually evaluate every aspect of your nonprofit.

Chapter Two includes a benchmarks assessment to help identify infrastructure issues needing work. An infrastructure based on the core elements increases the likelihood that the board-level committee structure and the staffing divisions of the organization cover all the critical components necessary for success.

Develop a Variety of Funding Methods

If you are too dependent on one event, government grant, or major donor, your nonprofit can fail. No more than 20 percent of your funding should come from any single source. If that major source of funding dries up, the nonprofit may not be able to continue providing programs. Use a variety of fundraising strategies, but first identify the pros and cons of each. (See chapter 3 of *Nonprofit Management Simplified: Programs and Fundraising.*)

Don't forget to do an assessment of all your fundraising strategies annually. What is the cost of conducting the fundraiser compared with the net profit? Include in those costs volunteer and staff time. Focus on a few well-done fundraising strategies rather than a wide variety of strategies that burn out volunteers and staff with little financial return.

When you look carefully at successful nonprofits and their fundraising strategies, you will find that they usually have two or three strategies that they have fine-tuned to the point where the community eagerly awaits their events. The Salvation Army's Christmas kettles and bell ringers are a great example of a fundraising strategy that has been used successfully for more than a hundred years.

The sample "Fundraising Costs for All Resource Development Strategies" shows the various fundraisers of an actual nonprofit and the relationship of income to their cost. The monthly fundraisers were wearing out the volunteers and donors, and they became more and more hesitant to participate. And the biggest fundraiser, the Rubber Ducky Race, took the most time and resources but had a small financial return. A simple assessment showed the leadership what the problems were, leading to some changes in their approach to fundraising.

Train the Board and Staff on Roles and Responsibilities

Good-hearted folks often join boards of nonprofits out of a strong sense of altruism. However, few board members and staff have received training on how to work together, lines of authority, how to conduct effective meetings, and their various roles and responsibilities.

In fact, in my more than three decades working with hundreds of nonprofits, I can count on one hand the number of boards that have received training in their roles and responsibilities. And since many in the sector either have social worker degrees or enter the sector from the for-profit world, few executive directors—or staff—understand their roles in relation to the board.

If you have worked in nonprofits for very long, you know that in spite of your best recruitment methods, a toxic board member can wreak havoc within the board. A mutant-ninja-turtle board member is an apt description of such board members: You never know how they will respond to any given situation, either attacking like ninjas or being extremely slow like turtles, and being virtually ineffective as board members.

Decrease the potential for toxic board members by building and implementing solid recruitment, training, recognition, and dismissal policies and procedures (chapters 2 and 6 of *Nonprofit Management Simplified: Board and Volunteer Development*).

Questions to Answer

Before the necessary incorporation paperwork, articles of incorporation, and bylaws are filed with the state and federal agencies, make sure you understand all laws and regulations associated with nonprofits. Some states and countries, for example, have fundraising registration requirements; others tax property of nonprofits, etc.

And some basic questions should be answered by the founding board members. Nonprofits are less apt to fail if these types of questions are asked and answered clearly before start-up.

Use these questions as a guide to help you decide if you should go ahead with starting a nonprofit or if it would be better to work with an already-existing nonprofit to help expand its programs in order to include coverage of issues that you believe are lacking in the community. Include your answers in the details of your business plan when appropriate.

If you are an existing nonprofit but struggling, take the time to answer these questions to see if you can identify the issues behind the challenges you are facing.

Needs/Resources Analysis

◆ What are the current needs in the community for the particular services of the anticipated nonprofit?

◆ What other nonprofits or state agencies are already addressing similar needs?

◆ Could their programs be expanded to incorporate the newly identified needs?

◆ How will your nonprofit fill any identified gaps in needs?

Vision/Mission Clarification

◆ Why do you want to start the nonprofit?

◆ What is the passion or ultimate dream (vision) you want to accomplish?

◆ What specific services or programs will your nonprofit do?

◆ How will you fulfill the mission and vision?

◆ You should be able to state both the vision and mission in twenty-five words or less.

Board of Directors

◆ Who are the stakeholders that need to be a part of your start-up governing board? *Although the IRS does not require that you have more than one board member when you file your articles of incorporation, I strongly recommend having at least eleven committed individuals who are willing to spend the time and money to start the nonprofit.*

◆ Do potential board members understand their legal obligations, conflict-of-interest issues, and liabilities?

Legal Requirements

◆ Do you know the necessary legal forms (city, county, state, and federal) to complete for becoming a tax-exempt or a tax-exempt/tax-deductible organization?

◆ Does your city, county, or state/country require a solicitation permit or charitable registration?

Resource Development

◆ What are the potential sources of funding for your nonprofit? Is your development plan realistic?

◆ What are the budget needs?

◆ Who are your competitors for funding?

◆ Do you anticipate no more than 20 percent of your funding coming from any single source?

◆ Have you established a statement of your fundraising ethics (e.g., no coercion, proper allocation of fundraising costs, etc.)?

Administration

◆ What type of accounting system will be needed as well as policies and procedures related to the receipt and disbursement of funds?

◆ What insurance needs will you have, such as directors and officers liability insurance?

◆ What type of facilities and staff are you going to need the first year, the second year, etc.?

◆ What kind of personnel policies/benefits will you need?

◆ What kind of database management system, programs, computers, and networking systems will be needed?

Volunteer Development

◆ How many volunteers (board, committee, and program) will be needed?

◆ How will board members be recruited, trained, and recognized?

◆ How will program volunteers be recruited, trained, dismissed, and recognized?

◆ What role will board-level committees play in your governance?

Marketing

◆ What is the image or brand identity of your nonprofit that you want to convey to stakeholders, funders, potential funders, etc.?

◆ How will you market that image?

◆ How will you publicize events and programs?

Programs

◆ How will you establish effective programs?

◆ How will you measure the effectiveness of the outcomes of the programs?

◆ What types of research mechanisms will you need to track outcomes?

◆ How will the outcomes improve the community as a whole or impact the identified mission of the organization?

◆ Are there governmental laws or regulations that will impact program implementation?

◆ Will you need to do criminal background checks on volunteers, board members, and/or staff?

Community Involvement

◆ What role will the nonprofit play in the community?

◆ How will the nonprofit become known as the expert in your particular field of service?

◆ How will your nonprofit collaborate with other nonprofits with similar missions?

Strategic Planning

◆ What's the business plan for the nonprofit for the next three to five years in all the areas listed?

◆ How will the plan be updated on an annual basis as part of a strategic planning process?

◆ How will the nonprofit respond to unexpected changes in the environment in which the programs operate?

Develop a Written Business Plan

As the old cliché states, "Failure to plan is planning to fail." Start-up nonprofits often have general ideas of what they want to do but do not take the time to put together a business plan. Longtime nonprofits are so busy executing programs that they believe they don't have time to do planning. Both approaches can eventually destroy the nonprofit.

Sample Business Plan for Year One

Community Child Abuse Prevention Center

Vision: All children in our community are safe from sexual abuse.

Mission: To educate the community, develop effective programs, and support the victims of child abuse.

Values: Equal treatment for all. . . children should be safe. . . voluntarism is the best way to initiate change, etc.

Slogan: An Open Door to Love

Marketing and Resource Development	Programs and Community Involvement	Administration and Volunteer Development
A three-year marketing plan will be developed that will increase brand identity by 30 percent.	A community-wide collaboration of agencies addressing similar issues will be convened within one year.	Necessary papers will be filed for incorporation as a 501(c)(3) organization.
A three-year research plan will be developed that will allow for ongoing responses by stakeholders and the general public to brand awareness strategies.	A community-wide needs and resource assessment will be developed, with the collaboration partners as stakeholders.	A paid executive director will be hired within two years.
Within one year, all material used by the agency will reflect brand identity strategies and logo.	The agency will be a catalyst for the development of a community-wide plan for reducing the number of child abuse victims.	A system of internal financial controls will be developed and implemented for testing within a year.
A three-year fundraising plan will be developed that will increase financial resources by 30 percent per year.	A written plan for each program will be submitted to the board within the next three months.	The board will be expanded to twelve members by the end of the year.

Marketing and Resource Development	Programs and Community Involvement	Administration and Volunteer Development
The number of grants written will increase 25 percent per year.	Each program will develop three- to five-year plans for implementation of outcomes measurements strategies.	A detailed policies and procedures manual will be developed within two years.
A planned giving program will be established, with the first $100,000 bequest within two years.	Criminal background checks will be done on all staff and volunteers before they are hired or become involved with the nonprofit.	Board-level committees will be appointed to address administration, board/volunteer development, programs, community involvement, marketing, and resource development.
		An accounting firm will be recruited to handle the finances, or a fiscal agent will be recruited until the IRS designation.

To lessen the possibility of failure, an individual considering starting a nonprofit organization needs to take the time to develop a plan. The entire process for developing the initial business plan does not have to take more than four hours. This plan then becomes the basis for an ongoing strategic planning process.

Once these questions are answered satisfactorily, you are ready to file the articles of incorporation (**Appendix B**), complete the bylaws (**Appendix C**), and put together a business plan, as shown in "Sample Business Plan."

The business plan for a nonprofit does not need to be complicated. In essence, it is really your first strategic plan.

The business plan template is based on the "Core Elements of a Successful Nonprofit" and the "Organizational Structure Based on Core Elements."

Once the start-up board has agreed to the organizational structure and all the questions have been answered satisfactorily, you are ready to file the paperwork to become a tax-exempt organization.

Evaluate Legal Requirements and Submit Documentation

Nonprofit organizations in the United States are defined by state corporate law and the IRS. A review of state and federal laws related to nonprofit incorporation in your county or state is an essential first step in becoming a nonprofit. State and federal laws for nonprofit incorporation are usually posted online. As the first step in evaluating legal requirements, print copies of the laws and make sure your nonprofit meets the requirements.

If you were unable to place a check mark beside each of the IRS guidelines, write down why not. Once this assessment is complete, present it to members of your start-up board of directors so they know whether or not the nonprofit will be able to meet these characteristics and if there need to be any changes in your approach to starting the nonprofit.

These are the characteristics of a nonprofit as defined by the IRS in the United States. Place a check mark beside each characteristic that the proposed nonprofit will meet. The author's clarification of the guideline is in italics.

❑ Incorporated under state law as nonprofit.

❑ Exempt from state taxes (*depends upon state law*).

❑ Tax exempt and able to receive tax-deductible contributions from federal income taxes under the IRS Code 501(c)(3).

❑ No part of the net earnings inures (*goes*) to the benefit of or is distributed to its members, trustees, officers, or other private persons.

❑ Reasonable compensation for services rendered.

❑ Distribution of funds for the purposes of the nonprofit organization.

❑ No substantial part of the activities is for carrying on of propaganda or otherwise attempting to influence legislation. (*This limits legislative activity but does not prohibit lobbying. Although "substantial" is not defined by the IRS, it is recommended that no more than 20 percent of the organization's budget be spent on lobbying.*)

❑ The organization cannot intervene in any political campaign of any candidate for public office. (*Do not support any political candidate; to do so could jeopardize your nonprofit status.*)

❑ There shall be no engaging in activities or exercising of powers that are not in furtherance of the purposes of the corporation. (*To do so could trigger unrelated business income taxes.*)

❑ Upon dissolution of the corporation, assets shall be distributed for one or more exempt purposes.

❑ There may be a financial surplus, but it shall be used only for exempt purposes.

❑ The income from the sale of services or products shall go only for the exempt purposes.

definition

Remember, it can sometimes take up to a year before you receive your tax exemption from the IRS. The *IRS Data Book* for fiscal year 2012 shows that the IRS approved 87 percent of the 501(c)(3) applications. One-quarter of 1 percent of the applications was denied, and slightly less than 13 percent of applicants gave up and withdrew their applications.

So while you are waiting, consider operating under another nonprofit with a similar mission. It could serve as your fiscal agent and handle donations you might receive while waiting for the official designation.

Oh, and one other thing. Be sure you understand the various governmental categories of tax-exempt, tax-deductible organizations and then submit your information for the correct one. There are several types of nonprofits listed under the 501(c)(3) category, so make sure you apply for the one that best matches your vision and mission.

To Recap

◆ Do your homework and research whether or not there is a need for the nonprofit.

◆ Recruit and train a board of directors.

◆ Determine primary sources of funding.

◆ Answer basic questions satisfactorily.

◆ Develop a one-year business plan based on the core elements organizational structure.

◆ Submit legal documentation to governmental bodies.

Chapter Two

Evaluating the Nonprofit

IN THIS CHAPTER

- ⋯➔ Rationale for Core Elements Assessment

- ⋯➔ Benchmarks by which board and staff can compare their progress toward management and organizational excellence

- ⋯➔ Strategies for using the assessment to jump-start a strategic planning process

- ⋯➔ What the board and senior staff know about the nonprofit

I'm following the advice of an old mountain woman who said: "When I walks, I walks s . . . lowly. When I sits, I sits loosely. And when I feel a worry coming on, I just go to sleep." (Author unknown.) Too many executive directors "go to sleep" when they "feel a worry coming on" about how well their nonprofit is doing.

Assess the Six Core Elements

Frequent assessments are a must for any nonprofit. Assessments will provide you with the data you need for strategic planning, program evaluation, outcomes measurements, adherence to the vision and mission, and evaluation of all six of the "Core Elements for a Successful Nonprofit" as shown in **Chapter One**: Administration (legal compliance, financial management, risk management, facilities and equipment, human resources management, etc.); board/volunteer development (recruitment, training, recognition, dismissal); resource development (fundraising, grants, planned giving, etc.); marketing (brand, publicity, marketing strategies, etc.); programs (program plans, outcomes measurements, research, etc.); and community involvement (collaborations, partnerships, etc.)

The six core elements provide an easily identifiable basis for assessments, building a solid nonprofit infrastructure, and increasing the possibility the nonprofit will succeed. A simple but effective way to assess the health of a nonprofit organization is for you to evaluate how well the core elements are being implemented in every aspect of the organization.

Using the core elements table below, on a scale of 1 to 10 (10 being "outstanding" and 1 being "poor"), rate how well you think your nonprofit is doing in each of these areas:

Core Element	Rating
Administration	
Board and Volunteer Development	
Resource Development	
Marketing	
Programs	
Community Involvement	
Total*	

*Out of a possible 60 total, if your score is 50 to 60, the nonprofit is doing very well, 30 to 49 is average, 10 to 29 is poor, and 1 to 9 is *help!* Look for scores in each element that are 5 or less to identify priority areas on which to focus attention.

Once the executive director has completed this rating of the organization, the rest of the staff and the board of directors can also do this simple assessment as a kickoff to the one-hour assessment.

Implementation of a wide-ranging variety of assessments can be done through focus groups, formalized research, telephone surveys, stakeholder surveys, and award programs such as the Malcolm Baldrige National Quality Award, based on Total Quality Management principles. Local city, county, and state governments, United Ways, and foundations can be good sources of environmental statistics and community research on social services issues since they often use such tools to determine funding priorities.

Information specific to your particular nonprofit is important. If your nonprofit, for example, deals with child abuse issues, you will need statistics and trends related to the abuse of children, treatment of offenders, and the community's economic trends that impact abuse. State agencies and other research groups are great sources of data on trends in the state.

Staff and volunteers can sometimes regard any assessments as indications that what they are currently doing is either incorrect or inadequate. It is important, therefore, that the assessment techniques you use are nonthreatening and identify areas of the organization's management and programs that need improvement. If the assessments are regarded as benchmarks rather than pass or fail grades, staff and volunteers are more apt to buy into them.

If you have not done strategic planning, or you are looking for a quick snapshot type of assessment of the organization, a one-hour assessment is a great way to help prioritize organizational issues that need to be addressed in the planning process. Such an assessment can lead to a strategic planning process, or it can be a part of the strategic planning process as

The nonprofit had been serving the needs of senior citizens for almost thirty years. But the demographics of the clients had significantly changed in the past five years: more clients with Alzheimer's disease, average age had increased from seventy-five to eighty-five, and donations were down. Yet the leadership of the nonprofit kept doing things the same way they had always been done.

Fortunately, a new executive director understood that change was needed and led the board and staff toward their first strategic planning session. Included in the preparations was an organizational assessment. As a result of the assessment, the board was able to successfully make shifts in programs and budget that reflected the identified environmental changes.

stories from the real world

outlined in *Nonprofit Management Simplified: Board and Volunteer Development.*

Conducting the One-Hour Assessment

There are a variety of ways you can use the "Core Elements Assessment" (**Appendix C**) as an organizational assessment:

- ◆ Only the executive director completes the assessment.

- ◆ All staff completes the assessment.

- ◆ The board and senior staff complete the assessment.

- ◆ Only the board members complete the assessment.

- ◆ Board members, senior staff, and primary stakeholders (such as major donors) do the assessment.

My experience using the Core Elements Assessment with hundreds of nonprofits has shown that having both the board and the senior staff do the assessment provides candid and useful results. If too many peripheral people (such as lower-level staff and stakeholders) do the assessment, it muddies the waters, since it is unlikely they would have the depth of knowledge to complete the assessment. The most effective way to do the assessment is for it to be mailed or emailed to board members with a deadline for its return. The senior staff can be given the assessment during a special staff meeting.

Be sure that you do not coach individuals taking the survey or give answers to anyone doing the assessment. That's because the assessment must be based on the perceptions of the people taking the survey. If, for example, board members do not know if the nonprofit has a vision statement, the problem might be a lack of communication to the board if there is, in fact, a vision statement. The results of the assessment from board and staff are kept separate since staff is usually more knowledgeable about the nonprofit than are board members.

For a simple analysis, look for categories with less than 50 percent of the statements checked, which could indicate a weak area. Also look for differences between staff and board responses. A tally sheet can be used as a more detailed analysis of the results and can be easily converted into a bar chart or wall chart.

Other Types of Assessments

There are many different types of evaluation tools or assessments that can help you know how well the nonprofit is functioning. The types of assessments include:

- ◆ Environmental or contextual analysis: What is the environment within which the nonprofit is operating, such as economic, demographics, geographic, ethnicity, philanthropic, and political?

- ◆ Internal assessments: A detailed analysis of all internal systems, policies, and procedures

- ◆ Board/staff assessments: How well do the board and staff understand their roles and responsibilities?

- ◆ Quality assessments: What is the level of quality for all internal and external services of the organization, i.e., Total Quality Management?

- ◆ Vision and mission assessments: What is the level of achievement or fulfillment of the vision and mission?

- ◆ Values assessments: What are the ethics or values of the nonprofit, and how well are they being implemented?

- ◆ Organizational goals and objectives: How successful is the nonprofit in fulfillment of board-approved goals and objectives?

- ◆ Program Outcomes: How well do programs meet specific outcomes measurements?

Example

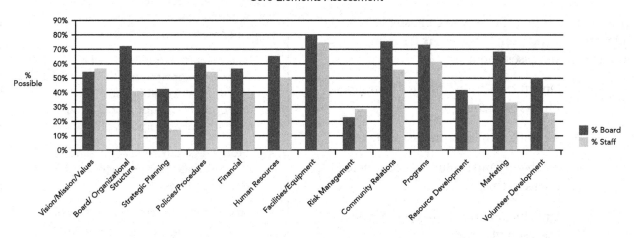

Use an Excel spreadsheet to enter the data and make a bar chart showing the differences between staff and board responses. The assessment should not take participants more than thirty minutes to complete, with an additional thirty minutes for you or one of your staff to enter the results into a database.

Remember, this is a benchmark assessment and should not be confused with, or substituted for, more detailed organizational assessments, such as internal financial audits. The Core Elements Assessment is for the sole purpose of jump-starting a year-round assessment process. Once the results are tallied, take time at the next board meeting to show the results so the board can decide what the next steps might be: a strategic planning process, a more thorough analysis, etc.

To Recap

◆ Choose the best assessment for your nonprofit at its stage of development.

◆ The Core Elements Assessment is a benchmark assessment that is best used with the board and senior staff.

◆ After doing the assessment, the board and executive director will have benchmarks by which to compare their progress toward management and organizational excellence in all the core elements.

◆ The Core Elements Assessment can be used to jump-start a strategic planning process.

◆ The executive director will have a better understanding of what the board and senior staff know and don't know about the nonprofit.

Chapter Three

Establishing Legal and Financial Management Structures

IN THIS CHAPTER

···→ Fiduciary responsibilities of board members

···→ Assessment of financial management systems

···→ Financial management policies and procedures

···→ Required legal documents

···→ Policies and procedures for facilities and equipment management

A checkbook and a shoebox full of receipts was the extent of the accounting system at my first nonprofit. As a result, one of my first duties as the new executive director was to set up an entire accounting system. This was in the dark ages before computers, so the only way I could figure out the financial situation was to do a handwritten debits and credits ledger for the previous year. And, of course, the ledger was written in pencil as my high school accounting teacher had taught me. She would have been so proud!

Truth be told, I kind of enjoyed playing detective by trying to balance the ledger right down to the penny. Some might have perceived building the previous year's debits and credits as a waste of time. But by the time I was done, I really understood the financial condition of the nonprofit.

As I moved to progressively larger nonprofits over a period of two decades, I was appalled to discover that all but one of them had significant financial management issues that were not being addressed. In fact, one of them had a $1.2 million deficit, and the board did not know it. And even though I was not an accountant, it did not take much work to identify the major problems: no written financial management policies and procedures and a lack of regular assessments of internal controls.

My experiences with the financial management systems of nonprofits, as both an executive director and a consultant, are not at all unusual. Many nonprofit executive directors are hired for their expertise in fundraising or in programs, but they may have little or no training in financial management. One of

An experienced nonprofit executive was brought into the community to guide the merger of two nonprofits. But the merger board had failed to look carefully at the financial management of both of the nonprofits. It turned out that the former director of one of the nonprofits had been borrowing from one federal grant to pay for the expenses of another federal grant: an illegal procedure. It took the executive director two years before the board was satisfied that the finances of the merged organization were straightened out. And, by the way, that did not happen until the board decided to fork out the money to hire a CPA to head up the accounting division of the new, merged organization. The original accounting staff did not have the skills it needed.

Example

the more common college degrees for nonprofit executive directors is a master's degree in social work. But rarely has someone with an MSW degree taken accounting courses.

In larger nonprofits, there is often an expectation that other staff will take care of management areas in which the executive director does not have training. In smaller nonprofits, however, the executive director must often handle many management functions that might ordinarily be delegated to other staff: finances, risk management, board and volunteer development, marketing, etc.

Or the new executive director, after a cursory look at the internal operations, sees what the director thinks must be a good accounting system since it has been in use for a long time. Relieved to not have to deal with financial issues, the director makes the mistake of focusing attention on other aspects of the organization, avoiding the monitoring of staff designated to handle all financial procedures.

If you neglect to take a detailed and frequent look at how the finances of your organization are handled, it can eventually be disastrous not only for you but for the nonprofit. Many times, staff in the finance or bookkeeping position is good at giving reports but deficient in the actual accounting methods.

Fiduciary Responsibilities of Board Members

Nothing will cause a board of directors to meddle in an executive director's administrative responsibilities more than problems in the financial report, audit, or other financial issues. To fulfill its legal fiduciary responsibilities, the board must be assured that the proper financial controls are in place.

The standards of accounting for nonprofits in the United States include benchmarks that board members can use to make sure the nonprofit is fiscally sound.

There are several financial management assessments that board members can use to assure themselves that the nonprofit's financial controls are in place:

◆ Internal audit

◆ Financial policies and procedures checklist

◆ Audit checklist

While it is the responsibility of the executive director to monitor and verify the execution of financial strategies and policies, responsible board members understand that they have a legal and ethical responsibility to periodically review the financial policies and accounting system. It is unusual for problems such as embezzlement to occur if board members put in place the essential monitoring strategies that will assure them that all financial aspects of the organization are in order.

Board members can get a report on the internal financial processes by having the volunteer treasurer, or other board officer, at least annually do an internal audit. If you want to ensure solid internal

Internal Audit Checklist

Date audit completed:_____

Person doing the audit:_____

Procedure Number	Action Audited	Yes	No	Comments
1	Invoices are reviewed by check signatories when the check is signed.			
2	Invoices are approved by appropriate staff.			
3	Invoices are correctly coded by nonprofit division/ program, per the chart of accounts.			
4	Invoices are filed and easily retrieved for verification.			
5	Accounts receivables are coded to proper accounts.			
6	Invoices (accounts payable) are paid within thirty days of billing date.			
7	Billings and donor reminders (accounts receivables) are prepared and mailed at least quarterly.			
8	Billings/donor payments (accounts receivable) are verified at least quarterly and indicate correct program or division.			
9	Bank accounts are reconciled monthly.			
10	Bank reconciliations are reviewed and approved by the executive director.			
11	Electronic transfers are verified and coded correctly.			
12	Interest income is coded correctly.			
13	Bank statements are filed and easily retrievable.			
14	Month-end budget/financial reports are run by the fifteenth of the following month.			
15	Payroll tax deposits are made each payday.			
16	Copier and postage use is recorded and billed to the proper programs at least monthly.			
17	Equipment invoices are copied and filed in equipment folder.			
18	Financial reports are reviewed by executive director before presentation to the treasurer and board of directors.			
19	W-4s and I-9s are completed and filed for all new employees.			
20	Random petty cash audits are documented.			

infrastructure, take the time at the beginning of your tenure, and at least quarterly, to review the accounting procedures. A simple internal audit checklist can be a great tool to immediately identify problem areas and should take about thirty minutes to do.

Some executive directors use this type of internal audit as a way to assure their volunteer treasurer that the right internal controls are in place. Or, depending on the type of accounting system, have the auditor assist you in the development of a checklist that is better suited to your nonprofit. Either way, periodic, random checks of the financial controls are absolutely essential for any nonprofit.

Job Description: Administration Committee or Internal Operations Committee

Responsible to: Board of directors

Purpose of committee: Development of policies; monitoring of year-round internal controls for management excellence.

Key Responsibilities

◆ *Planning*—Develop goals and advise staff on implementation.

◆ *Resource and needs assessments*—Assess community, volunteer, staff, and internal resources available.

◆ *Finance*—Develop and monitor policies and procedures for internal financial management that conform to standards of accounting and meet governmental regulations and requirements.

◆ *Legal*—Develop and monitor legal policies and procedures that prevent harm to volunteers, staff, and the organization.

◆ *Facilities*—Provide for the procurement, upkeep, and policies related to the facilities.

◆ *Technology/equipment*—Evaluate and procure suitable equipment.

◆ *Human resources*—Develop and monitor policies and procedures related to employment of staff.

◆ *Risk management*—Annually review the insurance needs; develop safety and disaster plans and policies.

◆ *Board communications*—Keep the board of directors informed on implemented strategies, results of administrative efforts, and any potential policies needed.

Committee Structure

The chair of the committee shall be a member of the board of directors and shall select, or cause to be selected, a vice chair. The chair and vice chair shall also serve as members of the executive committee and shall keep the board informed on the committee's oversight of board-approved committee goals. A majority of the committee shall be board members. Subcommittees or short-term task force groups may be formed to complete the committee's objectives. The treasurer and assistant treasurer shall be members of the committee.

Time Commitment

At least one meeting per month or as needed to fulfill the committee's goals.

Note: In smaller communities, consolidation of administration and board/volunteer development committees is feasible.

Example

Do not notify the staff that an internal audit is going to be done; otherwise, they will have time to make changes. The internal audit is meant to be an examination of the day-to-day routines of staff in the priority procedures of financial management.

A finance committee, or a subcommittee of the administration committee, can play a key role in helping you hold the staff accountable for the financial controls and in providing assistance to the board-appointed treasurer. Develop a job description for the treasurer based on the responsibilities outlined in the nonprofit's bylaws (**Appendix B**).

Review the job description of the administration committee or internal operations committee. One of the responsibilities of this committee is to monitor the financial management of the nonprofit. If the nonprofit is dealing with some particularly difficult financial issues, the administration committee could establish a task force to deal with these issues and report back to it on its progress in dealing with the issues.

I cannot emphasize enough how helpful a volunteer-driven approach can be, especially if you lack an accounting background. Not only does this type of committee act as a buffer between you and the board, but by putting individuals on the committee who are knowledgeable about financial matters, you benefit from their expertise.

By using a financial checklist, the committee or individual board members can assure themselves that the proper policies are in place and are being followed by designated staff.

Any orientations for board members should include an overview of financial processes and policies as well as training on how to understand financial reports and audits. It is the responsibility of board members to review and approve the annual audit. This responsibility begins with their selection and approval of an auditor.

The size of your annual budget determines the type of audit needed: a compilation, a financial review, or a full audit.

The board is responsible for the hiring of the independent auditor. Give at least three CPAs an opportunity to bid on providing the annual audit, particularly those with nonprofit audit experience. To

---

Financial Checklist for Board Members

Check those items that you can answer "yes" to:

❑ The board has a standing committee designated to oversee finances.

❑ The designated committee makes at least quarterly reports to the board of directors.

❑ At least two signatures are required on all checks over a designated amount.

❑ Receipts are given for all cash contributions.

❑ Staff develops the annual budget, with finance committee and treasurer's assistance and review.

❑ Treasurer's reports are written and are easily understood.

❑ Treasurer's reports include balance sheets, budget, and variances between revenue and expenses (monthly and year to date).

❑ Investment and banking policies are regularly reviewed.

❑ An audit or financial review is performed annually and is unqualified.

❑ The accounting system is evaluated regularly by the board and adheres to current US standards of accounting for nonprofits.

❑ Accounting books are easily accessible to board members and are located in a secure place.

❑ IRS 990s, I-9s, payroll taxes, and other legal government documents are filed and easily accessible when required.

❑ The nonprofit has a positive fund balance, including a three- to six-month operating reserve fund balance.

Example

provide consistency, the bid process could include a request for a two- to three-year audit and completion of necessary state and federal reports, such as the IRS 990 and the 5500 pension report.

However, the same auditor should never be used for more than five years. This is because using the same auditor for a long time can lead to complacency in procedures. New auditors bring new eyes to the review of the financial management procedures.

Unfortunately, too many board members do not understand audits and are hesitant to ask questions and show their ignorance. The audit should be reviewed first by the administration/finance committee in a meeting where the auditor is present, and then the audit and the committee's report should be taken to the board for approval.

Establishing Financial Policies and Procedures

The establishment and maintenance of financial policies and procedures will help greatly in assuring the board of ongoing financial accountability. **Appendix D** is a sample of financial policies and procedures. A review of these policies with the auditor can help any organization solidify the procedures and policies needed for the critical financial controls.

> ### Audit Questions for Board Members
>
> To help board members understand the types of issues they need to look for when they are handed a copy of the audit, provide them with a checklist like this one, or ask the auditor to provide a list of questions:
>
> ❑ Was the auditor's examination conducted in accordance with generally accepted auditing standards for nonprofits?
>
> ❑ Is the information in the financial statement presented fairly in accordance with generally accepted accounting principles?
>
> ❑ What are the fund balances in separate funds; how have they changed since last year?
>
> ❑ What is the extent of, and reason for, interfund borrowing?
>
> ❑ Has the auditor supplied a management letter? If so, what are the recommendations? If not, why not?
>
> **Example**

After the auditor has given approval of the drafted policies and procedures, they should go to the board for approval. The approved document can be included in the policies and procedures manual, which should be reviewed annually by staff. It is recommended that copies of the financial policies be included in the board manual handed out during orientation.

A financial management checklist of standards, based on the "Core Elements Assessment" included in **Chapter Two**, can keep the essential benchmarks front and center for the finance committee. Based on the "Sample Financial Policies and Procedures" in **Appendix D**, the checklist will help you know if all the proper policies have been approved by the board of directors. The checklist should take about fifteen minutes or less.

Finally, you should complete the board member responsibility checklist in chapter 1 of *Nonprofit Management Simplified: Board and Volunteer Development* to verify that you understand board members' fiduciary responsibilities, and then give it to board members to complete during their orientation.

At least every other year, the treasurer should do a five- to ten-minute overview of board members' fiscal responsibilities as a reminder to each board member.

Legal Documents and Policies and Procedures

An additional fiscal responsibility of board members is to verify the annual filing of all required legal documents. Nonprofits will need to verify all legal requirements in their county, state, and federal governments.

For example, in the United States, the following documents must be filed:

IRS Form 990 or 990-N

The 990 form provides information on revenue, expenses, and the balance sheet. The completed form analyzes why the nonprofit would not be classified as a private foundation (which has different reporting requirements). Churches are not required to file the form unless they have unrelated business income (such as day-care facilities). Deadline for filing is the fifteenth day of the fifth month after the end of the fiscal year. A fiscal year is defined as a board-designated period of 365 days, such as a calendar year or any other period (e.g., September 1 through August 31).

Nonprofits with incomes of $25,000 or less must file the 990-N. Any nonprofit that fails to file the form by the deadline can lose its nonprofit status. Those organizations may not find out until the next January 1, when they're notified they have to pay taxes on donations they thought were exempt. And it could be months before their nonprofit status is restored. Congress required the form when it amended the tax code in 2007. It is estimated that thousands of small nonprofits lost their tax-exempt status because they either did not know about the requirement or they forgot to file it.

The 990 form is a public document and must be made available to anyone who requests it, although you can charge copying costs to the person asking for it. I always gave copies of the 990 to those who requested it for free, as a service to our donors. Nonprofits that are hesitant to give out copies of their 990 forms often have something to hide, such as exorbitantly high executive pay. Or, instead of making copies, include in your annual report the following statement: "Copies of our IRS 990 form can be viewed at our website, *guidestar.com,* and our state's regulatory agency." Not every state makes the 990 available on its website, so check first before adding the statement to your annual report.

Federal Form 990-T

Nonprofits with unrelated business income must file this form. Filing dates are the same as for the 990. Unrelated business refers to any sales- or income-producing program or event that does not fit with the mission of the nonprofit. For example, an organization providing job training for severely disabled individuals can have a lawn maintenance program where it trains its clients on job skills, since the purpose fits with its mission. However, a nonprofit whose mission is to mentor youth could not operate an adult day-care center without paying unrelated business income taxes, since the day-care center does not fit with its mission.

Federal Form 5500-C

The form provides information on the legal compliance and status of group benefit plans provided by the nonprofit for employees. The form is

---

Questions board members should ask when reviewing the treasurer's report include:

◆ Does the financial report include a balance sheet, and does the balance sheet show total cash on hand in all accounts?

◆ Does the balance sheet show the amount in cash reserves for operational expenses? *There should be a minimum of six months' cash available to cover operational expenses.*

◆ Does the report show the budget compared with the actual income and expenses for the time period (monthly, quarterly) and compared with the previous year's report for the same time period with percentage variances? *Any variances of 5 percent or more should be explained with a written report.*

◆ Does the report show the year-to-date income/expenses compared with the budget and not just for the budget period, with explanations of variances of more than 5 percent?

Example

meant to show that the pension plans are solvent and that carriers are putting away sufficient funds to cover potential claims. The filing date is the last day of the seventh month after the fiscal year ends.

State and Local Requirements

Requirements will vary from state to state or province to province, so it is critical for you to verify what needs to be filed. There may be city or county registration as well as fundraising and solicitation requirements.

State and federal tax codes change constantly, so it is always helpful to either have your nonprofit's accounting done by a CPA who is obligated to know about such changes or periodically check with a nonprofit attorney about any changes in the laws or reporting requirements.

Sample Legal Documents (United States)

◆ IRS Form 990 or 990N

◆ IRS Form 990-T

◆ Federal Form 5500-C

◆ Charitable registration (state and/or county)

◆ Solicitation permit (county or city)

◆ Property tax or inventory report

Example

Do you know where important legal documents critical to the organization are kept? If the committees need information on what the bylaws say, for example, about the role of the finance committee, it should be easy to locate the document. A periodic check on the location of important documents will verify that the files are in order, but it will also send a strong message to the staff that even the smallest detail is important. Be sure that the originals of legal documents are kept in a secure, fireproof location, such as a bank safe-deposit box.

You can use the "Legal Documents Checklist" as a starting point for developing a list of legal documents that fit your nonprofit. At least every other year an inventory of the documents should be taken to make sure the documents have not been moved or destroyed. The checklist should indicate not only if the document is filed somewhere but also where it is filed. A copy of the completed checklist should be included in your policies and procedures manual

---

Legal Documents Checklist

Nonprofit:_____

Date: _____

Your name:_____

Indicate with an "x" the documents you have and list the location. Add to the list as additional items are found that need to be saved indefinitely. Dates of most recent reviews or updates are also helpful. Delete any items not applicable.

Document	Location/Date of Last Review
❑ Annual reports	
❑ Board minutes	
❑ Bylaws	

Document	Location/Date of Last Review
❑ Vision statement	
❑ Mission statement	
❑ Values/doctrines list	
❑ State charitable solicitation registration	
❑ Current operating budget	
❑ IRS tax-exemption letter	
❑ Articles of incorporation	
❑ Financial audits	
❑ Insurance policies (bond, health, life, liability, personal injury, property, directors and officers, etc.)	
❑ Incorporation papers	
❑ Corporate seal	
❑ Leases and/or deeds	
❑ Personnel policies	
❑ Personnel files for each employee	
❑ Equipment service contracts	
❑ Tax forms (city, state, federal 990 or 990-N, 5500 pension, I-9, W-4, etc.)	
❑ Copies of IRS 990 for past seven years	
❑ Policies and procedures handbook	
❑ Inventory file	
❑ Board member files (past and present)	
❑ Employee benefits policies	
❑ Historical information	
❑ Other documents: ❑ _____ ❑ _____ ❑ _____	

Policies and Procedures Manual

Internal problems often arise when staff and volunteers are not clear on the proper procedures to follow. Policies approved by the board frequently wind up buried in past board minutes and are difficult to find when a situation arises where the approved policy is needed for decision-making.

If you develop a policies and procedures manual or handbook, easily accessible to volunteers and staff, it can be an invaluable tool for solving such problems. Such a manual is also helpful as a training tool for new staff.

One of the easy ways to keep the manual updated is to have a lengthy staff meeting once a year whereby the manual is reviewed page by page, with all staff present. It is during this meeting that staff determines whether the same procedure is being used, if policies are still relevant, or if there have been any policy or procedure changes that need to be added.

In a small nonprofit, where staff works across many divisions, placing copies of the manual on everyone's desk or computer can help eliminate confusion and decrease the number of times staff come to you with questions. Putting the manual together may take a while, but if a consistent format is used and it is readily available on the computer, changes can be made quickly when needed. The first manual can be developed by having each staff person complete a procedures page for every task performed, no matter how routine or mundane.

One of the techniques you can use to motivate staff to develop the manual is to remind them of what I call "The Mack Truck Theory of Management," which says, "If I get hit by a Mack truck tomorrow, I want to be sure someone can step into my place and easily perform my duties."

A suggested checklist of possible contents for a policies and procedures manual is included as **Appendix E**. Program-specific procedures or other items that require consistency in operation or implementation should be included in the manual.

> ### Policies and Procedures Manual Page Format
>
> ◆ Date: When the policy was written and approved by the board
>
> ◆ Department: List of all departments impacted by the policy or procedures
>
> ◆ Name: Person who wrote the policy or procedure
>
> ◆ Needed resources: List of forms, money, equipment, or people needed to do procedure
>
> ◆ Timeline: List of dates and tasks to complete in order to do the procedures, such as setting up board meetings
>
> ◆ Policy/procedure: Step-by-step detailed list of procedures or the board-approved policy statement
>
> ◆ File path: Location on the computer of the document/policy/procedure for use in making future changes.
>
> **Example**

Articles of Incorporation and Bylaws

Besides filing the articles of incorporation with the IRS when submitting the application for tax-exempt status, most states require that original copies of the articles of incorporation (**Appendix A**) and bylaws (**Appendix B**) be filed with the secretary of state. Amendments or changes to the bylaws, along with an updated list of the board of directors, should be filed with the appropriate state department when revised.

The bylaws of any nonprofit organization should be reviewed at least every other year to ensure their continued compliance with state and federal laws and to verify the organization is adhering to the mission. To ensure compliance, the bylaws should also be reviewed by an attorney, preferably one specializing in nonprofit or corporate law.

It is recommended that every new board member receive a copy of the bylaws. You can make sure each member receives a copy by including it in a board manual presented during orientation. It is a good idea to ask board members to sign a form stating they have read the bylaws and reviewed the manual.

Facilities and Equipment

One of the biggest investments nonprofits make is in their facilities and equipment. Yet, often there are no inventory procedures that must be in place for depreciation of the assets in the audit. Some basic standards for facilities and equipment management are included in the organizational assessment in **Chapter Two**. Additional issues, such as accessibility, safety, and maintenance, are included in **Chapter Five**.

To Recap

◆ Board members need to be educated on their responsibilities related to the audit and financial controls.

◆ The accounting system should meet the basic standards of accounting for nonprofits.

◆ Financial policies and procedures must meet all legal requirements.

◆ Legal documents should be easily accessible and filed appropriately.

◆ By setting up a policies and procedures manual, staff and board members will know what the proper procedures and policies are that they must follow in the fulfillment of their responsibilities.

◆ Facilities and equipment policies and procedures should be established.

Chapter Four

Evaluating Your Personnel Management

IN THIS CHAPTER

···➔ The reasons for personnel management policies and procedures

···➔ Hiring, training, orientation, recognition, and dismissal policies and procedures for all staff

···➔ Essential components of an employee handbook

···➔ The legal risks associated with personnel management

···➔ Components of a legal employee handbook

I was the new executive director looking through the personnel files of the fifteen employees. I was surprised to find that none of the files contained copies of performance reviews. "Are they filed somewhere else?" I asked the office manager. "No," he replied, "we've never had performance reviews."

Some of the employees had been in their positions for more than twenty years. I had already discovered that one of the senior employees was ill-suited for his job in fundraising. He had never learned how to use a computer and had not been successful at raising funds. Since no performance reviews had ever been done with him, I could not fire him but had to move him to a different job until a performance history could be documented.

Because I had no written records on personnel, I was forced to delay any major promotion or firing decisions until the new personnel management system was in place.

Reasons for Personnel Management Assessments

There are at least four reasons why periodic personnel or human resources assessments are important:

Improve Time Management

Unless solid human resources policies and procedures are approved by the board and implemented by staff, you can find yourself spending a lot of your limited time addressing staff issues: hiring, firing, conflict resolution, discipline, etc.

Remove Emotional Responses to Human Resources Issues

Good policies and procedures remove a lot of the emotional response to human resources issues. Because altruism is so often a key factor for a person taking a lower-paying nonprofit job, nonprofits are sometimes sloppy about human resources strategies and policies for fear they will lose valuable employees.

Limit Legal Issues

Your nonprofit is less apt to end up in court dealing with discrimination in hiring or firing, sexual harassment, or other issues if you set up proper legal steps for each of those strategies through the development and implementation of good human resources policies and procedures.

Increase Employee Productivity

Good human resources policies and procedures help all staff understand what is expected of them. Without periodic performance reviews, staff has no guidance or goals and objectives on which to base its work. As a result, productivity can decrease, as can morale.

There is an often unspoken belief that anyone who works for a nonprofit would never sue. Wrong. Nothing will cause the demise of a nonprofit quicker than a sexual harassment, sexual abuse, or wrongful-termination lawsuit.

Unfortunately, if you are like many nonprofit executives, you may have little or no training in personnel law. As a result, it will be easy to make preventable mistakes in hiring, firing, and personnel management. If you have not yet taken a course in personnel law, sign up for a class as soon as possible. The labor departments of most states offer periodic classes in labor law. Labor laws vary from state to state and country to country, so it is critical that you understand the laws in the state/country where you are working.

If you are serving in a larger nonprofit, it might be tempting for you to assign total responsibility for personnel management and training to a staff person. It is critical, however, that you educate yourself and the staff on human resource issues. That way, everyone can recognize potential problems before

---

Human Resources Management Standards and Checklist

❑ Personnel policies are maintained and evaluated regularly and are verified in compliance with state and federal employment laws.

❑ Personnel files are maintained on all staff in a secure location.

❑ Personnel files are accessible only to designated supervisors, the employee, and designated board members.

❑ All staff is annually reviewed and evaluated by the executive director or the designated supervisor.

❑ The stability and consistency of management staff is demonstrated by low turnover.

❑ Written job descriptions and salary ranges are available for all staff.

❑ If there is no paid staff, job descriptions and board expectations of volunteers are written and agreed upon.

❑ If there is no paid staff, evaluations of administrative volunteers are done by designated board members based on written expectations, policies, and procedures.

❑ The administrative budget includes funds for staff and volunteer training and professional development.

❑ The organization has a written affirmative action policy that clearly states it will operate without discrimination in the selection of board members, volunteers, and committee members, and in the employment of staff.

❑ A formal process is established and followed for the annual review or evaluation of the executive director (covered in chapter 4 of *Nonprofit Management Simplified: Board and Volunteer Development*).

Example

they bring harm to the nonprofit. Human resources laws change periodically, so make sure you and your designated staff include regular human resource training in your planning calendar.

This chapter should not be regarded as a comprehensive list of all the issues related to human resources management but, rather, a starting place. *Always check with an attorney familiar with employment/labor laws in your state and country when developing policies and procedures.*

Human Resources Standards/Benchmarks Comparison

Take the time to do a quick review of some basic standards or benchmarks, which will help jump-start the human resources strategies in your nonprofit. This simple review will help you set the stage for more detailed evaluations. These standards are based on the Core Elements Assessment in **Chapter Two**.

Put a check mark beside the statements that apply to your current human resources policies and procedures. Any items that are not checked indicate a need for some assessment and rework to meet the standards.

Assessment of Hiring Practices

This section will deal primarily with the evaluation of the hiring practices of the employees of a nonprofit. Human resources policies and procedures for the executive director are included in chapter 4 of *Nonprofit Management Simplified: Board and Volunteer Development*, since the board is primarily responsible for executive director recruitment, supervision, and evaluation.

Prepare for the human resources assessment by collecting the following documents:

◆ Job descriptions for all paid staff

◆ Salary/wage ranges for all staff

◆ Summary of all benefits available to all staff

Once all the documents are collected, answer the following questions:

❑ Do all staff positions have job descriptions that incorporate all the categories listed in the example?

❑ Are salary or wage ranges included in the job descriptions?

❑ Are salary ranges, wages, and benefits evaluated at least every other year and comparable to those paid to staff in similar-sized nonprofits in the community?

❑ Are all positions identified as either "exempt" or "nonexempt?" *Note: This issue is currently being discussed in the US court system, with some legal opinions stating that even exempt employees are owed overtime payment, so check with an attorney before finalizing these definitions.*

❑ Is an objective scoring system used to prioritize resumes?

❑ Are all interviewers trained in proper interviewing procedures?

❑ Are procedures written as to the hiring process?

❑ Are follow-up letters or emails sent to everyone who submitted resumes?

❑ Does the budget include funds to pay for costs associated with interviewing individuals outside the community?

❑ Does the budget include adequate funds to cover all salaries, wages, and benefits, including (at a minimum) annual cost-of-living increases?

❑ Are statements of understanding given to all new hires?

❑ Are the accounting and payroll departments notified immediately when someone is hired or fired?

Job Descriptions

Job descriptions, salary ranges, and benefit packages need to be developed and approved by the board of directors before the staff is hired. These issues are the responsibility of the board to guarantee the fulfillment of its fiduciary responsibility to make sure there is enough money in the budget to support staff costs.

Salary ranges for positions can best be developed by first drafting job descriptions for each position. The responsibilities of the position will determine if the position is exempt or nonexempt, at least per the labor laws in the United States.

"Exempt" is a position that is exempt from overtime reimbursement, or a salaried, management position. A "nonexempt" hourly-wage position means that any hours worked over forty per week are subject to overtime payment by law. In most states, if an employee is paid hourly, the employer is required to provide with a one-hour meal break for every eight hours worked, plus a fifteen-minute break every four hours.

Any employer who does not ensure the wage employee takes the time off work as required by law may be subject to overtime payment at time and a half. There have been cases where employees filed lawsuits and won overtime payment long after they left the job. If payment of overtime wages is a frequent occurrence, be sure there is money in the budget to cover the payments.

Note that there are currently several court cases in the United States that contend exempt employees should also receive overtime payments, so check with a labor law attorney to make sure your policies reflect current laws.

Check with your state or country's labor department to get its definitions of exempt and nonexempt, plus any other human resources legal requirements. Determine if a position is exempt by reviewing the sample personnel policies in the employee handbook (**Appendix F**). And be sure your employee handbook is reviewed by an attorney familiar with human resources laws.

Do not make the mistake of trying to make all employees salaried to avoid paying overtime. Another tactic employers sometimes use is the hiring of "contract" employees to avoid paying benefits. Again, be sure the employee fits the legal definition of "contract employee."

Be sure that the payment of payroll taxes is done promptly and within the time frames required by state and federal governments. If they are not paid in time, your nonprofit could be subject to some hefty fines.

> ### Components of an Employee Job Description
>
> ◆ Title
>
> ◆ Reports to (supervisor)
>
> ◆ Responsibilities
>
> ◆ Exempt or nonexempt
>
> ◆ Skills and education required
>
> ◆ Salary or wage range
>
> **Example**

Once the job descriptions have been put together, contact other nonprofits of similar size in your community and get copies of their job descriptions and wage/salary ranges to use for comparison. Other for-profit or public sector businesses (like a chamber of commerce or a school district) can also be good sources of information on salary ranges and job descriptions that fit the cost of living for your area.

Salary surveys are another way to get benchmarks for wage/salary rates. There are a number of organizations that do salary surveys: the state department of labor, your national affiliate, The Chronicle of Philanthropy, Association of Fundraising Professionals, etc. Be sure to find out if benefits are included in the totals.

Sample Rating Scale for Resumes for an Administrative Assistant		
Score: "5" priority or excellent		
Responsibility	Priority Level	Score
Experience as administrative assistant	5	
Nonprofit employment	3	
Software knowledge	5	
Event planning	3	
Receptionist experience	4	
AA degree (minimum)	4	
Bulk mailings and/or emailings	4	
Total	28	

When a job description is being developed, remember that the document will be used as evidence if any legal disputes occur. In other words, if the job requires a specific skill and it is not included in the job description, the employee could file a wrongful-termination lawsuit if fired because of lacking the skill.

Before the Interview

Once the board of directors has approved the job descriptions and determined that the salary and wage ranges are compatible with the annual budget, prepare the advertisement for the position. Be careful what is said in the advertisement. Be sure it fits the job description. Avoid ethnic discrimination by stating, "knowledge of Spanish important," for example, rather than "only Hispanics should apply."

Having potential candidates submit resumes makes it easier to narrow the field of candidates by eliminating those individuals whose skills and experience do not match the job description.

Before looking at resumes, prepare a scoring sheet by which every resume is evaluated. For example, use a rating scale to evaluate resumes for an administrative assistant position based on the job description. Narrow the field of candidates down to five to ten people using the rating scale. Send applications to the top ten candidates.

Do reference and criminal background checks before offering the job to the final candidate. The use of an objective scoring system removes a lot of the subjectivity and, should a lawsuit occur, shows the court that every effort was made to be fair in the hiring practices.

Interviews

A great way to narrow the field of candidates further is to conduct telephone or online interviews. Use a predetermined set of questions for all interviews. The questions should focus on issues that will help the interviewer determine if the potential employee has the needed skills and is able to interact well with others in a difficult situation—in this case, the stress of the interview.

Never ask questions that could later be translated into a lawsuit for unfair hiring practices, such as:

◆ How old are you?

◆ Are you married?

◆ Do you have children?

◆ Do you intend to get pregnant?

◆ When did you graduate from high school or college?

◆ What is your sexual orientation?

Upon completion of the telephone interviews, candidates are again scored and the final three to five candidates determined. Establish dates and times for the interviews with the final candidates. Use the same approach in the face-to-face interviews with the final candidates as was used in the telephone interviews:

◆ No questions that would indicate age, sexual orientation, marital status, etc.

◆ Do include questions related to experience and qualifications for the job based on the job description.

◆ Do include questions that will reveal the candidates' communication skills.

Statement of Understanding for New Hires

Include in the statement of understanding the following items:

◆ Salary or wage level at when hired

◆ Completion date for a trial service period whereby the employee and the supervisor have a chance to see if the person will be a good fit with the organization (usually no more than ninety days)

◆ Dollar value of all benefits and date effective

◆ A statement indicating that the hiring is based upon the attached job description and the employee's resume and application are true and accurate

◆ A statement that protects the supervisor, such as: "All wages and benefits shown are subject to confirmation by the payroll department"

◆ A statement that the letter is a "statement of understanding" and not a legal agreement

◆ A statement that hiring is dependent on satisfactory criminal background and reference checks

◆ A statement that adherence to the employee handbook is a requirement of employment (attach a copy of the handbook)

Conclude with a place for the new employee and the supervisor to sign and date the statement of understanding.

Example

Assessment of Orientation Procedures

Once the job has been offered and accepted, give the person a prepared package of items that will answer most initial questions of new hires, including a statement of understanding.

Once the decision has been made on the hiring and the employee has signed the statement of understanding, give a copy of the statement to the accounting/payroll department so that the new employee is entered into the system and the statement is put into the new employee's personnel file.

The payroll department should give a packet of information to the new hire that includes the I-9, W-2 forms, and sign-up information for the benefits packages.

Send thank-you notes to the candidates who did not get the job. Keep their resumes and all the interview notes on file for at least a year in case the new hire does not work out.

Collect the following documents in preparation for the assessment of the orientation policies and procedures currently being used by the nonprofit:

- ◆ Benefits packages: a packet of information that includes applications for benefits, descriptions of the benefits offered and application process, and how to access them

- ◆ Personnel policies: a copy of the most recent, board-approved personnel policies or employee handbook

- ◆ Nonprofit information: a handbook or pamphlet describing the history, mission, goals, and objectives of the organization

- ◆ The most recent copy of the strategic plan

- ◆ Current orientation strategies: a list of all the orientation strategies used by all the supervisors who hire staff

- ◆ Staff trainings in the past year: a list of trainings or workshops staff attended in the past year and how it is determined who goes to which trainings

Evaluate these five documents and the human resources procedures by answering the following questions:

Assessment

Place a check mark beside each statement if you have written policies and procedures:

- ❏ The benefits package accurately reflects all the benefits available to all staff as well as easy instructions on how to access the benefits.

- ❏ The employee handbook has been reviewed within the last two years by an attorney familiar with state labor laws.

- ❏ The information on the nonprofit that is given to employees is up to date.

- ❏ A copy of the strategic plan is included in the packet of information for the employee.

- ❏ All the supervisors who do hiring use the same orientation strategies.

- ❏ Training sessions and workshops are budgeted for all employees.

- ❏ A written policy states how supervisors determine who attends trainings.

Employee Orientation Checklist

- ❏ Statement of understanding
- ❏ Benefits information
- ❏ Personnel policies
- ❏ Information on the nonprofit, such as:
  - ❏ History
  - ❏ Mission
  - ❏ Latest strategic plan
  - ❏ Organizational chart for staff and board members
  - ❏ List of employees and their current positions
  - ❏ Health, safety, and disaster plans
  - ❏ Program-specific issues and information

Example

❏ A written policy states how supervisors determine what training is needed by each employee.

❏ All employees who work with volunteers have copies of the volunteer development policies and procedures.

❏ All employees have regularly updated personnel files available only to the supervisor, the executive director, and the employee (upon request).

❏ The orientation of a new employee includes not only information on issues related to the specific programs or division where the employee will be working, but also broader information related to the nonprofit.

For example, the new employee needs to be introduced to other staff and shown to the designated workplace. The supervisor should make sure that lighting, chair, and computer keyboard levels are correct for the new employee to reduce workers' compensation claims.

A member of the employees' health and safety committee (**Chapter Five**) should take all new employees through the building, pointing out escape routes and explaining the role the committee plays in building a safe and healthy workforce.

Verify the new employee has received the benefits packet and an employee handbook. Remind the employee to sign the last page of the handbook and return it to the supervisor.

If the new staff person will be working with volunteers, verify that they have a copy of the board-approved volunteer development plan, including recruitment, training, orientation, and dismissal policies for all volunteers. Other items to include in the orientation are listed in the example above.

Personnel Files

It is the supervisor's responsibility to make sure the human resources department has set up a personnel file for the new employee. Include in the personnel file the items indicated in the sample checklist in the "Sample Personnel File Checklist" (see opposite page).

One of the most effective and important legal defense strategies is the employee's well-kept personnel file. It is the responsibility of the executive director or human resources director to periodically do random checks of the personnel files to make sure they are in proper order and are up to date.

Staple the checklist to the inside of every employee's personnel file. When random checks are done, the actual contents of the file can be checked against the list of essential enclosures.

Performance Reviews

Sometimes employers do not do performance reviews or evaluations of their staff for fear they will quit their job. Failure to do annual performance reviews is one of the major reasons nonprofits have problems with staff. Whenever new staff is hired, they should be told that performance reviews are a part of being on staff. Most reviews are done at the following times:

◆ At the end of the trial service period, usually ninety days

◆ Six months after hiring (This allows enough time for the employee to get acquainted with the job. At this point, job objectives/goals can be set for the next year.)

◆ One year after hiring and every year after that

◆ At designated times if there are performance problems to be corrected

Sample Personnel File Checklist

Nonprofit:_____

Date of last file check:_____

Employee: _____

A check mark beside an item is an indication it is included in the file.

Item
❏   Hire date
❏   I-9 form
❏   W-4 form
❏   State new-hire form
❏   Job description
❏   Resume
❏   References
❏   Criminal background check
❏   Statement of understanding or contract
❏   Signed agreement page of employee handbook
❏   Charitable contribution form (used for workplace charitable campaigns, such as United Way)
❏   Performance evaluation, supervisor notes, and employee response
❏   Memos related to wage or salary changes
❏   Other: _____

If employees expect reviews and are allowed to give feedback to their supervisor, not only in response to the review comments but also on how well the supervisor is supervising, a sense of personal growth becomes a part of the process rather than the review being something to dread.

Training

One of the important issues that should be a part of any employee orientation is training on "Board and Staff Roles, Responsibilities, and Lines of Authority" in **Chapter Six**. Failure on the part of both staff and board members to understand this issue can have devastating and frustrating results. Without this training, staff may feel that if a board member suggests something, they are required to do it. Without this training, board members might meddle in staff responsibilities.

Training for nonprofit staff is often hit and miss or is based on how much money is in the budget. One of the best ways to develop employee skills is to do a very detailed analysis of the employees' job descriptions as a tool for establishing training strategies, "Job Description Analysis."

Although the project can take several months (depending on the number of employees), the result can be a prioritized listing of the organizational core competencies, a simplified way to evaluate the working relationship between supervisors and staff, and identification of the staff training needs. The results of the project are much more objective if the work is done by an outside consultant familiar with nonprofits and human resources management.

Job Description Analysis

The steps for analyzing job descriptions for the training analysis include:

Review Job Descriptions

Using a spreadsheet, a listing is made of every skill or knowledge needed for every job based on the job descriptions. If the same skill or knowledge is needed for more than one position, the number of times the skill/knowledge appears is shown on the chart.

Rate Skills/Knowledge Needed for Each Job Description

Using a form like the one in the chart, each supervisor rates the skills/knowledge for each job description (column 2) based on the level needed for the job. A copy is then given to the employee to fill in column 3 with the scores that indicate what the employee feels is the employee's current level of skills/knowledge. The supervisor, on a separate sheet, rates what the supervisor feels is the actual level of skill/knowledge for the current employee in the position (column 3). The form completed by the supervisor and the form completed by the employee are sent to the consultant for analysis.

Prioritize Skills/Knowledge

Based on the number of times a skill or knowledge is listed and the total of all the "needed" ratings, the list is prioritized. The result is a listing of the most important and most frequent skills and knowledge needed for the organization, or the core competencies for the organization.

Job Description and Development of Core Competencies

Agency: Date:

Job title: Employee #:

Form completed by:

*1 = very little or none; 5 = essential or all that is needed

1. Skills/Knowledge Needed (from Job Description)	2. Degree of Skill/ Knowledge Needed (Rated by Supervisor)	3. Current Level of Skill/ Knowledge (Rated by Supervisor)	4. Current Level of Skill/ Knowledge (Rated by Employee)	5. Difference Between Supervisor and Employee Ratings	6. Type of Training Needed
Employee benefits					
Personnel records					
Project management					
Claims management					
Enrollment transfers					
Vendor management					
Insurance billing					
Benefits record keeping					

1. Skills/Knowledge Needed (from Job Description)	2. Degree of Skill/ Knowledge Needed (Rated by Supervisor)	3. Current Level of Skill/ Knowledge (Rated by Supervisor)	4. Current Level of Skill/ Knowledge (Rated by Employee)	5. Difference Between Supervisor and Employee Ratings	6. Type of Training Needed
New employee paperwork					
Employee termination records					
Job description maintenance					
Employee evaluations					
BA or 1–2 years experience					
Analytical					
Written communication					
Verbal communication					
Time management					
Basic mathematics					
Common sense					
Reasoning					
Problem solving					
MS Windows 95/NT					
MS Word					
Excel					
Email and Internet					
HR software					
Statistics					

Instructions:

Supervisor—In column 2, rate every skill listed in column 1 as to the degree of importance in job fulfillment. If there are other skills or knowledge that are not listed, add them at the bottom of column 1 and rate them in column 2. Give a copy to the employee. On a second copy, complete column 3 and 6 and return the form in a sealed envelope to the Personnel Department.

Employees—In column 4, rate your level of skill/knowledge compared to the level of importance rating done by the supervisor in column 2. In column 6, indicate what training you feel would benefit your work experience. If there are additional job skills/knowledge you believe you use in your job that are not listed, add them on the bottom of column 1 or on the back of the form. Return the completed form in a sealed envelope to the Personnel Department.

Identify Individual and Organizational Training Needs

Combining the results from the supervisor and employee forms, the consultant can then do an analysis of the skills and knowledge training needed by each employee as well as compare the supervisor and employee ratings.

Assessment of Resignation and Firing Procedures

The staff turnover rate in nonprofits is high, with the estimated length of employment less than three years. Reasons for that include low pay, lack of adequate benefits, or burnout from the stress (particularly in agencies dealing with abused or at-risk individuals).

But turnover is expensive. Training time invested in an employee (usually six months to a year) does not begin to pay for itself until the second or third year. It is important, therefore, that the executive director attempt to identify the reasons why staff members resign in order to develop preventive strategies for other employees as well as to periodically evaluate the procedures used in handling firings and resignations.

By answering the following questions, the executive director will be able to determine in about thirty minutes if the correct policies and procedures are in place for employee resignations and firings:

◆ What is the rate of turnover of staff in all positions for the past five years?

◆ How many of the staff resigned, and how many were fired within the past five years?

◆ What were the top three reasons for the resignations or firings?

◆ What process or procedure is used when a staff person resigns?

◆ What process or procedure is used when a staff person is fired?

Exit Interviews

An exit interview can be a great way to ask some pointed questions of staff who are resigning. Since the employees are leaving, they are usually more apt to be candid than they would be if they thought their job was at risk. Some sample questions to include in the exit interview are shown in the example.

If the proper procedures are used in the hiring process, firings should be few. But even the best hiring practices do not guarantee someone will not have to be fired. Be sure, however, before firing an employee that appropriate laws have been followed related to documentation of performance problems. Although most states allow employers to "hire and fire at will," caution is always warranted before firing someone.

Verify frequently that all supervisors are following all disciplinary policies and documenting everything as they implement the human resources policies.

Every nonprofit should have access to an attorney who specializes in employee/employer law. Do not hesitate to consult an attorney before firing someone.

Sample Exit Interview Questions

◆ What have you enjoyed most about working at this nonprofit?

◆ What have you least enjoyed about working for this nonprofit?

◆ What could we have done to prevent your resignation?

◆ What suggestions do you have for improving employee relations and supervision?

Example

A new executive director discovered that none of the employees had ever had performance reviews. After several months, it became clear that one of the employees, who had been at the nonprofit for twenty-five years, was not at all suited for her position. Word somehow got out to the board that the employee's job was in jeopardy.

Because she was so well liked, board members were irate that the new executive director would even consider letting the employee go. Since the employee had never had a performance review, and in order to prevent a major problem, the executive director was forced to train the individual for a totally different position rather than fire her. Not the ideal situation, but one that solved the problem until a performance history could be documented.

Example

Another word of advice: always be sure to keep the board chair aware of any human resources issues or conflicts. This is particularly important if the employee to be let go is well liked by board members. It is the responsibility of the executive director, or the director's designated staff, to hire and fire employees, but firing an employee without carefully taking into consideration every ramification (such as the board members' opinions) can be very painful for the executive director and for the nonprofit.

It is always a good idea to have someone else present as a witness when an employee is fired. That way, there is a witness to what is said should a wrongful-termination lawsuit occur. Keep detailed notes on how the firing was handled and put them in the employee's file. Upon termination, walk the employee to the workspace, and watch as the employee cleans out the desk, returns the office key and other nonprofit property, and leaves the office. Sometimes it is necessary to change the locks to the office and to also change passwords on the computer if the firing was particularly difficult.

Be sure the fired employee's personnel file includes the details of the firing, both the how and why. What is in the file will be used in the event of a wrongful-termination lawsuit.

Never ignore the firing when talking to the other employees. Without going into any details, the supervisor or executive director can provide a succinct statement to employees, such as: "Susie Jones is no longer employed at our nonprofit. We will do everything we can to fill the position as soon as possible so as not to put additional work on each of you."

Assessment of Staff Recognition Strategies

It is easy for the executive director to assume that the wages and salary paid to staff are enough recognition. Sometimes volunteer recognition plans are more important than formal recognition of the hard work of employees. The development of staff recognition strategies can boost morale, but it can also motivate staff to continue working hard, especially when the nonprofit is short of staff or funds. An assessment of the staff recognition strategies can be done by asking the following questions:

◆ In what ways does the executive director recognize or reward staff efforts?

◆ In what ways do employee supervisors recognize or reward staff efforts?

◆ Is money in the budget for staff recognition programs?

◆ How can the nonprofit improve the way the staff is rewarded or recognized?

It is true that the most frequently desired recognitions by employees are bonuses or pay increases. But nonprofits are notorious for paying employees low wages and salaries to direct the most funds possible to the programs. But low pay is one of the main reasons why employees resign. So if you want to keep good

A simple recognition strategy that can pay big dividends is for the executive director to collect a lot of different types of sticky notes and stickers from the local office supply store. Every time the executive director notices a staff person going the extra mile to help a client, another employee, or a volunteer, the executive director puts a note on the employee's desk with a simple acknowledgment like: "Job well done!" "I appreciate your hard work," "So glad you are a part of our team," etc. Just be sure to keep track of who gets what notes and try to give similar recognition to every staff person at some point during the year.

Example

employees, make sure that salaries and wages are at least comparable to similar pay in the community for similar work.

And if regular performance reviews are tied to salary increases, it will not only encourage better performance but will also be viewed as a form of recognition of the efforts of the staff.

Equally as important is the avoidance of paying exorbitant salaries, which takes away from funding for programs but can also set the nonprofit up for very negative publicity if the high salaries are made known to the public.

A good rule of thumb is to have no more than a $10,000 to $20,000 difference between the next level up in the employee hierarchy. If employees know that the executive director is making twice as much as the senior vice president, for example, it can cause resentment. And even though such information is supposed to be kept confidential from other employees, rarely is it.

Be sure the board is supportive of the executive director efforts to increase employee pay. Sometimes even the most experienced business or corporate CEO who sits on the board is resistant to increasing the nonprofit's employee pay. The most egregious example of this was when the chair of the board of a local church—who happened to be a millionaire—was overheard telling a new member, "We keep our pastor poor to keep him spiritual."

The same attitude is often present among nonprofit board members who believe that employees who work for a nonprofit must be willing to accept low pay out of a spirit of altruism. Employees of nonprofits also have families and financial responsibilities. To force nonprofit employees to accept low pay puts unnecessary stress on the employees and their families, which is why they often resign and move to better-paying jobs.

Employee Recognition

There are a variety of types of recognition that can be used for staff, such as project recognition. If, for example, a staff person was put in charge of a particular project or event, the executive director and/or supervisor can make sure the employee's efforts are verbally acknowledged at staff meetings, board meetings, or the annual meeting.

Be sure notes are put into the employees' personnel files of any special recognition and are also mentioned in their performance reviews. Good recognition of project effort requires alertness on the part of the supervisor and executive director. It is easy to get so wrapped up in the flurry of personal duties that acknowledgment of the efforts of others is ignored.

For nonprofits with staff who have stuck with them through the good and bad times, consider putting together some type of recognition for length of service. United Way, for example, uses logo pins with various colored stones to recognize service for five years, ten years, etc. Make the pin presentation a big part of the annual meeting or the annual staff retreat. Again, make sure to keep track of who gets what pins and when.

Employee Handbook Assessment

One of the most important documents a nonprofit has is the employee handbook or personnel policies. State and federal labor laws can change every year, so annual updates of the handbook are critical and should be reviewed by an attorney familiar with labor laws and nonprofits.

It is possible to do a one-hour assessment of the employee handbook by putting a check mark beside each standard listed in the sidebar. A sample employee handbook that contains examples of policies based on these standards is in **Appendix F**.

Checklist for Employee Handbook Standards

The employee handbook includes policies and procedures related to the following issues:

❑ Frequency of handbook reviews by an attorney

❑ Employee signature indicating the employee has read and agrees to adhere to the policies in it

❑ Employee training strategies

❑ How and when human resources policies are changed

❑ Types and nature of employment (full time, part time, exempt, nonexempt, etc.)

❑ Equal employment and nondiscrimination

❑ Personnel files (what to include, control of files, updates)

❑ Employment of relatives

❑ Immigrant hiring

❑ Conflicts of interest

❑ Outside employment

❑ Confidentiality of client, nonprofit information

❑ Overtime

❑ Reference and criminal background checks

❑ Performance reviews and evaluations

❑ Employee benefits

❑ Payroll issues: timekeeping, paydays, employee terminations, pay corrections, and payroll deductions

❑ Work conditions

❑ Leaves of absence

❑ Conduct and disciplinary action

❑ Nonprofit assets and business expenses

❑ Use of nonprofit supplies and equipment

 practical tip

To Recap

◆ Personnel management assessments can improve all aspects of HR.

◆ Standards help assess the HR management.

◆ HR management should include assessments of all policies and procedures for hiring, orientation, personnel files, performance reviews, training, dismissal, and recognition.

◆ Assessment of the employee handbook is necessary to ensure legal compliance.

Chapter Five

Implementing a Risk Management Plan

IN THIS CHAPTER

    ···➔ Type of insurance needed by the nonprofit and where to get it

    ···➔ Establishing cybersecurity policies and procedures

    ···➔ Procedures to build a workplace that will be safer, healthier, and more accessible for all employees, volunteers, clients, and visitors

    ···➔ How and when to respond to disasters, natural and man-made

    ···➔ Crisis communication policies

Risk management encompasses a wide variety of issues: insurance, man-made disasters, abuse of clients, lawsuits, workplace safety, natural disasters, and crisis communication. Risk management for nonprofits is not just about having adequate insurance but is also about reducing the level of risk for the nonprofit, the staff, the volunteers, and the clients by implementing prevention policies and procedures.

To be effective in your management of the nonprofit, include in your standard procedures a frequent examination of all the risk issues associated with your facility, programs, and the board, as well as the overall functions of the nonprofit, especially the financial controls.

When significant changes occur within your organization, or there are changes in programs, consider the level of risk and the impact that such changes will have on safety and insurance issues. It is the board's responsibility to make sure there are adequate policies and procedures in place to implement any changes, but it is your responsibility to propose needed policy changes.

To avoid potential lawsuits, train staff and volunteers on how to deal with safety issues as well as issues like sexual harassment and client abuse. They also need to know how and when to do criminal background checks on prospective employees or volunteers.

A youth pastor was arrested for the sexual assault of two young girls. The man had a history of sexual abuse and was listed in the state's public database as a sexual predator.

Unfortunately, the church does not have a policy that requires criminal background checks on potential staff and volunteers. Now the church is facing a lawsuit by the parents for failing to protect their children.

Even if the church has liability insurance, it is doubtful it would be protected from a lawsuit, since it failed to perform due diligence by doing a criminal background check on the individual before placing him in the youth director position.

 stories from the real world

Insurance

The best way to evaluate insurance needs of your nonprofit is to work with an insurance agent, preferably one who has nonprofit liability experience. Some chambers of commerce have small business insurance packages for their members, and it could be well worth the minimal expense to join the chamber to access the insurance package. If there are problems locating suitable insurance carriers, talk to directors of other nonprofits with similar programs and risk issues to find out what types of insurance they have.

Included in "Types of Insurance" (**Appendix G**) is a list of potential policies that should be considered in the light of a nonprofit's risk level. Not all nonprofits will need all the insurance packages. At a minimum, to protect the board and staff, directors and officers liability insurance is a must.

Although some nonprofits believe insurance is a luxury and the assets of the nonprofit are so small that insurance is not necessary, plaintiffs have been known to pursue the board members' personal assets when they find there are few assets in the nonprofit's coffers. Most states have Good Samaritan laws that protect volunteers, but check your state or country's laws so you know what is covered and what is not covered.

Smaller nonprofits are finding that the tenure of their staff, especially the executive director, will be longer than the two- to three-year average if some types of insurance, such as health and retirement benefits, are offered.

Larger nonprofits that have not revisited their risk management policies in a while may want to schedule at least every-other-year reviews of their insurance packages.

It is the responsibility of board members to evaluate the level and type of insurance coverage needed. Staff can help by doing the evaluation and presenting a report to the board-level committee assigned to administrative issues.

However, a board-level task force or committee should also be involved in the analysis of any insurance packages that impact the staff. If the board committee is working on the staff benefits issues, the results will not be based on any perceived conflict of interest on the part of the staff who might have prepared the report. If the board is involved, there is also a better chance that the costs of adequate insurance will become a part of the annual budget, as it should be.

An important aspect of liability policies is "defense costs outside the limits." If the cost to defend a claim is included in the policy limits, it may eat up the policy limits to the point where there is little or nothing to pay a judgment if awarded.

Finally, your nonprofit and board can be subject to suits for "failure to maintain proper and adequate insurance coverage." Coverage must be the issue, not price. All deliberations related to insurance should be noted in the minutes of the board meetings. Be sure to include in the minutes the names of individuals who voted against any insurance motions.

Potential policies related to insurance issues include those in the sample chart "Sample Insurance Policies."

Always remember that having insurance is no guarantee that the nonprofit will not be sued. This is particularly true with directors and officers' liability insurance. If the board fails to provide oversight of the financial policies and condition of the nonprofit, no amount of insurance will protect the board. I am not an attorney, so always remember to check with an attorney on legal issues like insurance.

Establishing Cybersecurity Policies and Procedures

The issue is not *whether* your nonprofit's information will be hacked, but *when*. Too many nonprofits are operating as though no one would ever do such a thing to them because they are doing good in the community. Wrong.

There are specific steps a nonprofit can take to increase its cybersecurity:

◆ Provide board and staff training on cybersecurity issues.

◆ Include cybersecurity on liability policies.

◆ Develop policies and procedures on how confidential and financial data will be handled to prevent hacking.

◆ Establish finance and/or audit committee(s) to regularly review all financial reports and procedures.

◆ Hire a security firm to do a cybersecurity analysis.

Example

The Points of Light Foundation decided a few years ago to test its cybersecurity. Within fifteen minutes, sitting in a car in the foundation's parking lot, the security firm the foundation hired was able to hack into its confidential information.

Some examples of policies related to cybersecurity include the following:

◆ At least annually, a data security expert will review the organization's vulnerability to hacking.

◆ Annual inventories will be conducted of all devices in order to prevent theft.

◆ The number of people with access to the organization's computer network will be limited to senior staff.

◆ Passwords for all networks and computers will be changed monthly.

◆ All software will be updated quarterly.

◆ All data will be backed up daily, with both a hard copy stored off-site and an electronic version stored on the cloud.

◆ Confidential client, employee, and financial data will be stored on a secure site, accessible only to designated supervisors.

Example

So how do you protect your data? What role does the board play in cybersecurity? What policies should you have in place?

Prevention is always the best strategy. Periodically take time (ten minutes) at a board meeting to discuss a cybersecurity issue or policy. Since a primary board responsibility is "due care," the board must develop policies that protect the nonprofit from breaches of confidential information and financial data. A board that does not do this is setting the organization up for increased liability.

The development of specific policies and procedures related to potential security issues will not only provide a fertile training ground for both board and staff but will also decrease the possibility that your nonprofit will lose credibility if confidential employee, donor, financial, or client information is hacked and stolen.

Recognizing and Preventing Abuse

Even the best insurance and the best policies and procedures are no guarantee that a staff member or a volunteer won't abuse children, youth, the disabled, or the elderly, or that they will not be accused of sexual harassment.

Sample Insurance Policies

Policy	Responsible	Resource
The board of directors will purchase directors and officers insurance.	Board	Insurance companies, chambers of commerce, other nonprofits, state associations of nonprofits
Insurance benefits for staff, such as health insurance, 401(k), etc., will be evaluated annually by the administration committee and any changes recommended to the board.	Board, finance, or administration committee	Insurance companies, chambers of commerce, other nonprofits, state associations of nonprofits
The administration committee will annually review insurance packages currently in use and determine if additional insurance is needed, making recommendations to the board. The staff will assist by doing a preliminary analysis and presenting it to the committee.	Board, finance, or administration committee, staff	Insurance companies, chambers of commerce, other nonprofits, state associations of nonprofits
Adequate insurance coverage will be included in the annual budget.	Board, finance committee	Insurance companies, chambers of commerce, other nonprofits, state associations of nonprofits
The state's Good Samaritan laws will be checked at least every other year to verify the nonprofit is in compliance.	Volunteer development or administration committee	State labor and volunteer laws

To effectively manage such risks, make sure all staff and key volunteers are trained in how to recognize possible abuse. If you suspect abuse or sexual harassment, deal with it immediately! Do not try to shove it under the rug or hope it will go away.

The nonprofit's staff is required by law to report any suspected abuse. To diminish the risk of such abuse, do criminal background checks on all staff and volunteers working with vulnerable clients. Even if a background check does not reveal any problems, it might mean a person has not yet been caught abusing. Pair staff and volunteers with experienced individuals for the first year so that someone is monitoring their behavior, especially when working with vulnerable clients.

Policies related to abuse prevention are included in the "Sample Abuse Prevention Policies" (see opposite page).

Employee Health and Safety Committee

An employee-run health and safety committee can be an invaluable tool for you to make sure the facility and grounds are safe and to encourage staff, volunteer, and clients in healthy lifestyles. Once the committee has done a complete safety check of the building, the committee can also be involved in the promotion of healthy workplace projects and the development of internal and external disaster plans. Providing opportunities for staff to have ownership of these types of issues can ensure that they will be more apt to be prepared in case there is a problem.

Recruit volunteers to serve on the employee-run health and safety committee. It will help the committee get started more quickly if you have already prepared a draft job description for the committee's review (see "Sample Employee Health and Safety Committee Job Description," page 50).

Sample Abuse Prevention Policies

Policy	Responsible	Resources
All staff and volunteers working with vulnerable clients will be trained on how to recognize abuse.	Executive director, human resources manager, volunteer development coordinator	State department of health and human services, nonprofits dealing with abuse issues
Staff or volunteers accused of abuse will be suspended until the allegations are investigated by the proper legal authorities and the individual is either cleared or criminal charges are filed. If cleared, the individual will be restored to employment and receive back pay for the suspension period. If charged, the individual will be fired and receive no back pay.	Executive director, human resources manager, volunteer development coordinator	State department of health and human services, nonprofits dealing with abuse, police
Criminal background checks will be conducted on all staff and volunteers working with vulnerable clients.	Executive director, human resources manager, volunteer development coordinator	Law enforcement or designated local or state agency responsible for conducting criminal background checks
All new staff and volunteers will be paired with an experienced person for the first year of their involvement.	Executive director, human resources manager, volunteer development coordinator, and the supervisor of the person	Staff and volunteer development policies and procedures

Include on the health and safety committee the staff person responsible for facility maintenance. The committee can review the job description, set objectives, and develop any needed policies. You can then take the draft policies to the board's administration committee, which will review them and make final recommendations to the board.

Besides the development of policy recommendations for the board, the duties of the health and safety committee can include facility and equipment analysis, accessibility assessments, building a healthy workforce, and disaster preparedness.

Facility and Equipment Analysis

Regardless of whether or not the nonprofit owns the facility or is renting it, upkeep, repair, and replacement are essential tasks. A "Facilities Maintenance and Safety Checklist" can be used as the basis for a safety and accessibility assessment by the employee committee.

The committee or a designee can do a walk-through of the facility, using the maintenance checklist, looking for worn or broken items that could be

The employee health and safety committee of a midsized nonprofit decided to set up a six-week challenge to see who could walk the longest distance and who could lose the most weight.

At the end of the six weeks, the executive director was given an award by the employees for "Walking the Farthest in the Most Pain." The executive director was facing hip surgery but refused to bow out of the competition. The employees demonstrated their appreciation for the executive director's leadership with the funny but heartfelt award.

stories from
the real world

Sample Employee Health and Safety Committee Job Description

Title: Health and Safety Committee

Responsible to: Executive director (or staff person responsible for internal operations)

Purpose of Committee: To develop policies and procedures that will provide a safe and healthy workplace.

Key responsibilities:

◆ *Safety*—At least annually examine the facility, equipment and grounds to identify potential hazards and accessibility issues and to make recommendations to the executive director for upkeep, repair, or replacement. Recommend training programs that will inform staff, clients, and volunteers on necessary safety procedures. Annually conduct fire drills and an inspection by the fire department.

◆ *Health*—Identify programs that will encourage healthy lifestyles for all staff, volunteers, and clients.

◆ *Disaster*—Develop an internal and external disaster plans and procedures.

Committee Structure

The chair of the committee will be appointed annually by the executive director. At least three staff will volunteer to serve on the committee. (Note: The number of people on the committee will depend on the size of the facility and the number of staff and clients.)

Time Commitment

At least one meeting per month or as needed to fulfill the committee's goals.

Example

a safety hazard if not repaired. Depending on the age of the facility, the walk-through could be done monthly, every other month, every six months, or annually.

Any identified problem should be brought to your attention so you can decide if it is something the janitor can fix, if it requires an outside contractor, or if it will require replacement.

Facilities Maintenance and Safety Checklist

Area/Activity	Daily	Weekly	Monthly	Responsible	Comments
Water Fountains					
Clean and sanitize		X		Staff	Appropriate cleaner used
Building Exterior (General Housekeeping)					
Clean cobwebs		X		Staff	
Dust columns		X		Staff	
Clean signage		X		Staff	
Wash glass windows and doors		X		Staff	
Wash trash cans			X	Staff	
Blow walkways	X			Staff	
Pest control			X	Contractor	

Area/Activity	Daily	Weekly	Monthly	Responsible	Comments
Check sound systems		X		Staff	When volume turned on for any event
Building Interior (General Housekeeping)					
Dust signage		X		Staff	
Check lighting and replace as needed			X	Staff	
Check doors and signage			X	Staff	
Check ceiling tiles for leaks			X	Staff	
Check door push bars			X	Staff	
Pest control			X	Contractor	
Clean tiled areas		X		Contractor	As needed
Vacuum carpeting		X		Contractor	As needed
Building, Safety, Equipment					
Check AEDs			X	Staff	
Check fire extinguishers			X	Staff	
Check emergency lights			X	Staff	
Dumpster area					
Clean area		X		Staff	
Clean gates		X		Staff	
Air conditioning					
Temperature regulation	X			Staff	
Filter replacement			X	Contractor	
Exterior lighting					
Check exterior lighting			X	Staff	
Poles, up lights, roof			X	Staff	
Clean window ledges			X	Staff	
Restrooms					
Cleaning	X			Contractor	Six days/week, staff checks
Supply replenishment	X			Contractor	Six days/week, staff checks
Pest control					
Check for bees, ants, or wasps		X		Staff	
Computer Systems					
Back up office systems	X			Staff	Backup drives switched daily

Area/Activity	Daily	Weekly	Monthly	Responsible	Comments
Update software virus and firewall protection			X	Contractor	
Update server software		X		Contractor	
Grounds Maintenance					
Mowing		X		Contractor	
Plant beds		X		Contractor	
Irrigation system inspection		X		Contractor	

As the executive director, it is your responsibility to make sure that the annual budget includes facilities and equipment maintenance and capital improvement line items so there is money to repair or replace items when necessary.

Include in the annual facilities assessment evaluations of access and exit points, especially if anyone involved with the nonprofit has a disability. Access issues cannot be ignored.

Religious organizations are not required by law to meet ADA (US Americans with Disabilities Act) Title II requirements in older buildings, but other nonprofits must make sure their facilities meet ADA requirements.

If your nonprofit has fifteen or more employees and one of them has a disability, ADA laws will apply. If any portion of the facility is rented to outside groups, ADA laws will also apply.

The health and safety committee should conduct an accessibility audit and then develop recommendations to make the facility more user friendly for seniors and the disabled. A search on the Internet for "accessibility audit" will provide a variety of audits that can be adapted to nonprofits.

The *ADA Compliance Pricing Guide, Second Edition* is a resource for financially prioritizing the upgrades to the facility that will fit within the nonprofit's capital improvement's budget. Be sure to take local building codes into account in any renovations and make sure any safety changes stay within fire codes. Local fire departments will often do free fire safety assessments.

The committee should also examine all equipment to make sure it is safe to use. Training should be provided to staff and volunteers on how to properly use equipment, especially equipment that may be a safety hazard, even something as simple as a paper cutter.

Ergonomically correct furniture can also be critical for the prevention of workers' comp claims. Workers' comp claims will be reduced if safety is a priority.

By the way, don't forget that any type of injury, no matter how minor, should generate a written injury report. Sometimes a minor injury can result in a workers' comp claim, so all injuries must be reported. The safety committee can make sure employees are trained on the proper steps to take to report any type of injury.

A Healthy Workforce

Healthy employees mean fewer sick days and greater productivity. Once the employee committee has completed its access and safety evaluation, the development of wellness programs for the employees can be addressed.

Regardless of the health issues, employee committees can develop creative, year-round programs that will encourage staff to improve their health. The local hospital is usually a good source for health and wellness strategies and workshops.

Sample Employee Health and Safety Policies

Objective	Policy	Responsible	Timeline
Safe work environment	An employee committee will be established by the ED.	ED and health and safety committee	Annually
Equipment and facilities upkeep	The committee is responsible for finding and reporting any items that need to be replaced or repaired.	Health and safety committee	Quarterly
Facilities upkeep	The committee is responsible for finding and reporting any items that need to be replaced or repaired.	Health and safety committee	Monthly
Cost	The board of directors will include in the annual budget line items for facilities and equipment maintenance, repair, and replacement.	Finance committee, board of directors	Annually
Healthy employees	The committee will develop training programs that will encourage healthy lifestyles for clients, staff, and volunteers.	Health and safety committee, human resources division	Annually

Internal and External Disaster Plans

It does not make a lot of sense to have all the insurance needed without making sure that the nonprofit has a disaster plan, and that staff and volunteers are prepared for disasters at the building (internal) or in the community (external). Every staff person should know exactly what to do in the event of a disaster, especially if the disaster hits when the nonprofit is open for business.

Make sure that regular (at least weekly) backup copies of all computer data are stored off the premises. Copies of all important legal documents, insurance papers, and inventory lists should also be stored off-site.

To assist in planning for disasters, review the suggested steps to take *before* a disaster hits:

◆ Get copies of your county and city disaster plans.

◆ Develop internal and external disaster plans compatible with county and city plans.

◆ Develop and sign any needed mutual aid agreements (also known as memorandums of understanding) to ensure cooperation between responders during a disaster.

◆ Annually review and update plans and agreements.

◆ Get a copy of the community's information and referral (I&R) disaster plan.

◆ Train members, staff, and volunteers on how to respond to a disaster.

Internal Disaster Plan

The employee health and safety committee can use the following list of tasks to help in the development of the nonprofit's internal disaster plan:

◆ Contact the county emergency management agency to find out which of these disasters are possible in your community and how best to prepare for them: tornadoes, hurricanes, floods, chemical spills, earthquakes, violence at the workplace, etc.

◆ Determine if the nonprofit has adequate insurance: coverage for loss of facility, loss of furniture, and loss of business; coverage for immediate relocation of the office and any rebuilding costs.

◆ Store important documents or copies of them off premises: computer files, legal documents, insurance papers, bank information, a copy of the most recent financial statement, donor lists, employee contact information, etc. By the way, this is much easier to do if you store these items in the Internet cloud.

◆ Emergency equipment to keep on the premises includes flashlights, batteries, generators if necessary, fire extinguishers, defibrillators, water, blankets, first aid equipment, etc. (The emergency management agency can give you a list of items to have on hand, as can the American Red Cross.)

◆ Establish a crisis chain of command: Allow for the fact that staff may also be victims. Communicate the emergency plan to volunteers, staff, clients (and their families), board members, etc. Give supervisors the home addresses and phone numbers of all employees. Contact information for key volunteers should be maintained at the homes of senior staff. Be sure emergency contact information for clients' families is stored off-site.

◆ Post in all rooms of the building a map showing evacuation routes.

◆ Annually review the disaster plan with staff and key volunteers. If you have vulnerable clients, be sure staff and clients knowing what to do in an emergency.

◆ Conduct regular fire and safety drills.

◆ Post emergency phone numbers at each person's desk: local disaster relief personnel, government officials, local shelters, police, fire, I&R program, American Red Cross, The Salvation Army, etc.

External Disaster Plan

Internal and external disaster plans require basically the same steps since there is no way of knowing ahead of time if the nonprofit's facilities will be impacted by an external disaster. Any involvement of your nonprofit in local disaster response will depend first on whether or not your facility has been damaged.

The most important thing to remember is: *All disasters are local.* This means that the immediate response to a disaster is always through local volunteers and charities. It can sometimes take several days before the debris is cleared sufficiently so that state and national disaster response and relief agencies are able to get to the disaster site.

There are three specific steps a nonprofit should take if and when a disaster strikes. The following steps must be a part of the internal and external plans when a disaster strikes:

Assess the Impact of the Crisis

Depending on the crisis, contact the following representatives to assess the impact and the needs being addressed by frontline disaster relief nonprofits and to coordinate communication. Post the contact information for each of these organizations in every office and off-site with senior staff and the lay leadership:

◆ Insurance company

◆ Emergency services

◆ American Red Cross

◆ Salvation Army

◆ Local information and referral

Determine Staff, Nonprofit, Community Needs

Contact the board chair and communicate the estimated impact of the disaster on the staff, the nonprofit, and the community. Activate an internal plan by having key staff determine the impact on staff and anyone inside the facility. If appropriate, activate mutual aid agreements. If needed, contact other nonprofits to see if they need assistance.

Activate the External Disaster Plan

Depending on the assessment of the disaster's impact, activate the appropriate actions from the disaster plan. It is critical to handle communications through the disaster relief nonprofits. *Do not attempt to do their jobs.*

If you decide that you want your nonprofit to be involved in helping members or community residents prepare for or recover from a disaster, the following hints will be helpful:

◆ Know what you can and cannot do to support relief agencies that come into the area.

◆ Make sure that you are prepared to take care of yourself and your nonprofit's volunteers, staff, and volunteers if the disaster impacts your nonprofit directly. The American Red Cross or emergency management agency can give you a list of recommended supplies to have on hand in the event of a disaster. Communicate that information to all staff and volunteers. If you are going to be assisting at a disaster, bring your own water, food, and shelter.

◆ If your nonprofit must have electrical power, be sure someone is trained on how to use a generator. Two of the most frequent causes of death are an improper use of a generator and electrocution from downed power lines.

◆ Train volunteers. Ask local relief agencies (American Red Cross, The Salvation Army, FEMA, etc.) to train volunteers who want to assist after a disaster. Training can include everything from first aid to how to make sure water is safe to drink, how to use a chain saw, how to use a generator, how to fill sandbags, etc.

◆ Dress appropriately. Work shoes are better than tennis shoes to avoid sprained ankles and punctures when walking over debris. Other items to take with you include sturdy work gloves; disposable face masks, bandanas, or items that can be used as face masks; emergency tourniquets, and cooling headbands (cool when dipped in water).

◆ Take the right tools. Tools needed for different disasters include flat shovels, buckets, mops, and rags for floods; chain saws, rakes, and brooms for hurricanes; and shovels, crowbars, and picks for earthquakes. Also, take a basic tool set with hammer, pliers, socket set, and screwdrivers, plus an electrical tester and a fire extinguisher. Large, heavy garbage bags, wheelbarrows, or other containers (such as large plastic buckets) are also used to dispose of debris.

◆ Identify yourself. Arrange ahead of time to get identification badges from the relief nonprofits. Often only authorized volunteers are allowed in a disaster area. Not only does identification allow volunteers into the recovery area, but it also helps prevent looters from entering the site.

Besides your nonprofit's internal and external disaster plans, probably one of the most useful plans to have at each employee's desk will be the I&R disaster plan. Information and referral programs are usually run by county governments or local United Ways and are invaluable repositories of information on services available in the community. A working relationship with the local I&R will be of great help in the event of a community disaster since the I&R will know where to reach the critical services because of its extensive database. The I&R often becomes the focal point for information during and after a disaster.

Your nonprofit should support already-existing disaster response nonprofits rather than interfere with their ability to respond.

Mutual aid agreements (or "buddy systems") establish backup plans for specific services between neighboring nonprofits in the event of an emergency or crisis. These agreements can delineate the role for the nonprofit after a disaster without interfering with service-providing nonprofits. The agreements usually require advance training and clear communications between staff or volunteers of all the responding organizations.

Do not interfere with disaster response nonprofits. To do so makes their work more difficult.

Crisis Communication

Finally, you should have a crisis communication plan to keep the board, the staff, and the community informed, and to respond to possible media inquiries. Rumors and innuendos will flourish unless the board immediately implements a crisis communication plan if a disaster or criminal events occur within the nonprofit.

An effective crisis communication plan includes the prompt and honest response to a negative situation. It doesn't wait for a crisis to force a response.

If there is no crisis response plan, the media will control the response, which can lead to the wrong people speaking for the nonprofit, an increase in rumors, and a scrambling on the part of the leadership for damage control.

Potential policies for disaster response include the items in the "Sample Disaster Response Policies."

A crisis communication plan should include the following elements:

◆ Spokesperson: "The chair of the board will serve as the designated spokesperson for all communications with the stakeholders and with the media."

◆ Procedures: "As soon as possible after a crisis has been declared, the board will meet (within twenty-four hours) to develop strategies to address the situation and to develop a media response (when appropriate)."

"A statement will be developed by the board that is factual and includes steps the nonprofit will take to address the situation."

Example

Sample Disaster Plan Policies

Issue	Policy	Responsible	Resources
Internal disaster plan	The employee health and safety committee will be responsible for developing the internal disaster plan and procedures.	Executive director	American Red Cross, County emergency management agency, The Salvation Army, the fire and police departments
Internal disaster plan	In the event of a disaster at the facility, the executive director or designee will implement the board-approved plan and notify the board chair as soon as possible.	Executive director or designee	American Red Cross, County emergency management agency, The Salvation Army, the fire and police departments
External disaster plan	In the event of a disaster in the community, the nonprofit will implement the board-approved external disaster plan and notify the board chair as soon as possible.	Executive director, health and safety committee, board chair	American Red Cross, County emergency management agency, The Salvation Army, the fire and police departments
Communication	In the event of any crisis, only the board chair and executive director are authorized to speak to the media on behalf of the nonprofit. Should they not be able to do so, the associate executive director and vice chair of the board will speak on behalf of the nonprofit.	Board, board chair, executive director	Marketing or media company
Communication	Before speaking to the media, the spokespeople will confer and develop written responses to the crisis. Such responses will occur within twenty-four hours of the crisis or as quickly as possible.	Board, board chair, executive director	Marketing or media company

To Recap

◆ Risk management strategies include frequent reviews of the various types of insurance to see what is needed for the nonprofit.

◆ Board-approved policies are needed to protect the organization, such as insurance policies, abuse prevention policies, employee health and safety policies, internal and external disaster preparedness, and crisis communication.

◆ An employee health and safety committee can help the nonprofit to reduce risk by building a healthy workforce, training employees on safety issues, and doing periodic accessibility surveys and equipment and facility audits.

◆ The development of internal and external disaster plans can help your nonprofit not only be prepared but also provide assistance within the community when there is a disaster.

◆ A crisis communication will help the board and staff know when and how to respond to negative publicity or other crises.

Chapter Six

Balancing Competing Demands

IN THIS CHAPTER

- ┄➔ Tools to help the executive director manage the workday around strategies for working with people, completing projects, and handling paperwork

- ┄➔ Ways to balance the various management strategies in spite of limited resources

- ┄➔ How to balance time-management strategies around the competing demands of the six core elements necessary for a successful nonprofit

I have thirty years' experience as a nonprofit CEO and consultant, but I have not always been an "excellent" manager, nor did my management strategies always result in operational management excellence. Maybe that's because management can, by its very nature, be a messy and chaotic process, regardless of what all the books say or how much experience you have. But when management is done right, stress is reduced and everything goes more smoothly.

You will spend large amounts of time dealing with people, and dealing with people can be chaotic and difficult. Each person you work with (staff or volunteer, donor, potential donor, board member, or program volunteer) has his or her own worldview, personality, and motivations.

When I first started in management, I was naive enough to think I could be an excellent manager and still have everyone like me.

We all want to be excellent managers, right? But wanting it and achieving it is not always the same thing. What does it take for any manager, especially the executive director, to achieve excellence? Is it just a matter of managing time better or reducing the workload?

Webster's dictionary defines excellence as "being superior in achievement," a valid goal for any nonprofit executive director or leader. But the flurry of activities, fundraisers, pressing personnel issues, problems with the board, lack of training, and overwhelming importance of programs can result in ineffective management.

Ineffective managers will cause nonprofits to struggle to achieve their mission. They will constantly be looking for funding and wondering why they cannot get or keep good board members and other volunteers.

Although the basic strategies in this chapter will work for any manager, the information is geared specifically to nonprofit executive directors. Concrete suggestions are included to help you make judicious use of your workday by grouping tasks and strategies into an ideal eight- or nine-hour day. It is a given that most executive directors work more than eight hours a day, so adapt the suggestions to fit your specific schedule.

By the way, if you find yourself consistently working more than nine hours a day, it is time to take a serious look at two issues: time management and delegation strategies.

I learned the hard way that the demands of nonprofit management are so great that I could easily work ten- to sixteen-hour days seven days a week. I found it difficult, initially, to force myself to prioritize and eliminate tasks that could be delegated to a staff person or volunteer or be put off to another day or that weren't really critical to doing what I was hired to do: manage the nonprofit. But once I figured out how to prioritize, balance demands, and use my time wisely, I was able to reduce my daily work time to nine hours, with ten- to twelve-hour days the exception rather than the rule.

Evaluate the suggestions and principles in this chapter to see if there are some ideas that can help you become an excellent manager and executive director. Remember, there is no magic pill that makes someone an excellent executive director. It is up to you to find the strategies that work best for you.

Since the focus of this guide is on practical ways for you to balance the competing demands of the workplace rather than on philosophical management techniques, there is no attempt to address important issues like life/work balance, personal and family time, etc. Although those issues are critical for every executive director, this guide focuses only on work-related issues.

Each section in the chapter begins with a true story of a nonprofit executive director that illustrates the key issues that regularly confront nonprofit managers. The details of each situation have been changed to protect both the executive directors and the nonprofits mentioned in the various scenarios.

The Circle of Management Excellence

I vividly recall the first time I was confronted with my lack of management skills and the challenges of being a newbie nonprofit executive director. A downturn in the economy had led to 26 percent unemployment in the community, resulting in alarming rises in drug and alcohol abuse, domestic violence, and child abuse. The challenges for the community and the nonprofit sector were immense, but I was naively convinced I had what it took to make a difference.

The nonprofit was small, with an annual budget of $150K, and just one staff person—me.

One month after accepting the job, I sat at my desk with my head in my hands. I was exhausted. Seven committee meetings in one day were just too much. "What in the world have I gotten myself into?" I asked myself. I wanted to be an effective, efficient, and excellent manager, but there were just too many competing demands on my time.

Although I had owned my own home-based business and had been a volunteer for years, and even though I was young and had an abundance of energy, the overwhelming magnitude of the management job facing me was now apparent.

How was I possibly going to be able to do everything: accounting, administration, marketing, fundraising, programs, and even the janitorial work?

As I sat back in my chair and thought carefully about what seemed to be insurmountable tasks, I realized I needed to figure out how to excel at two things if I was going to be effective:

◆ Time management

◆ Balancing competing demands

Now, after thirty years of working on those two management challenges, reading a lot of books, and attending numerous classes, it has become clear to me that being an excellent manager can best be illustrated by a series of circles.

The Circle of Management Excellence

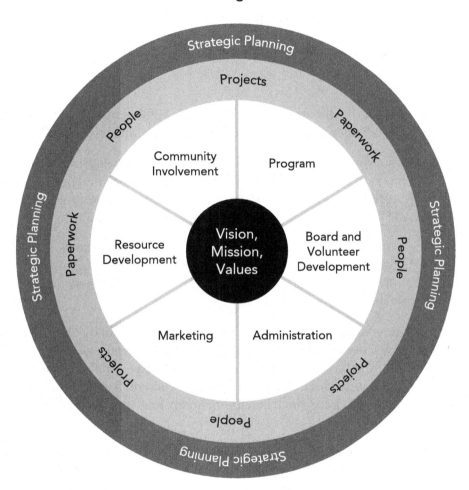

Strategic Planning

The outer circle of the wheel represents the responsibility of the executive director to lead a never-ending strategic planning process—not only for the organization but for your own personal management odyssey as well.

While you are guiding the nonprofit in the development and accomplishment of board-approved goals and objectives, there must also be a corresponding setting of goals and objectives for yourself on which your performance reviews will be based (chapter 4 of *Nonprofit Management Simplified: Board and Volunteer Development*).

No longer is it okay to do traditional strategic long-range planning, usually facilitated by an expensive consultant. Traditional planning processes focused on developing a three- to five-year plan but were often so detailed and unwieldy that when changes occurred in the environment in which the nonprofit operated, there was no way to adapt the plan to reflect the needed changes. And the plan was often out of date by the time it was completed. So it ended up sitting on the shelf until the next gung-ho executive director started a new strategic planning process and tossed the old one.

Modern strategic planning never ends and usually sets goals for no more than one to two years. It also includes specific strategies by which the nonprofit can quickly adapt to any needed changes between updates of the plan.

Using a simplified, annually updated, planning process will help you to manage your time by focusing blocks of time, projects, and people on the action plans for the annually updated goals and objectives (chapter 2 of *Nonprofit Management Simplified: Board and Volunteer Development*).

People, Projects, and Paperwork

The next circle of the wheel lists the three tools essential for the fulfillment of the strategic goals and objectives in any focus area of your responsibilities: people, projects, and paperwork.

Regardless of whether or not you are focused on marketing, resource development, or any of the other four core elements of a successful nonprofit, there will always be people issues, priority projects, and essential paperwork. If any task starts with you asking yourself, "What people, projects, and paperwork are needed for this?" it will be easier to allocate time-management strategies.

The Internet technologies now available can be invaluable to you in all these areas. For example, some great ways to expand community involvement and contact with a wide variety of people (whether locally, within a particular niche of service, or nationally), including blogs via social networks such as LinkedIn, Facebook, and Twitter, and emails.

Caution! It is easy to allow technology to run your life by getting into the habit of responding immediately to emails, blogs, tweets, telephone calls, etc. Balancing the use of technology also requires separating personal emails from business emails. If possible, delegate a staff or volunteer to screen telephone calls. Although it is more difficult to screen business emails, a good administrative assistant can really help you by letting you know which emails are urgent and which ones can be responded to at another time.

Computer technology can help you with tracking projects and paperwork through the use of project-management software. Especially helpful are software packages that tie the strategic plan into your project management, such as the WePlanWell or Envisio software.

Another hint I learned the hard way. When at all possible, limit unexpected telephone calls to no more than five minutes. If it looks like the conversation is going to take longer than five minutes, ask the caller if there is a convenient time for you to call back. Doing this allows you to control your time on the phone.

Core Elements

The spokes of the wheel are the six core elements, or focus areas, constantly demanding the nonprofit executive director's attention: administration, resource development, marketing, programs, community involvement, and board/volunteer development.

But all six of these areas must be balanced. For example, if you spend too much time in programs and ignore the administration component, eventually the programs will suffer. Or if you ignore marketing and branding promotion, it will be difficult to raise funds (resource development).

This balancing skill is especially important for executive directors of small nonprofits. Because your time can be so fragmented, by consciously focusing time slots on specific core elements, you decide what is important and when it is to be dealt with.

Vision, Mission, and Values

At the heart of any executive director's management excellence (the inner circle) are the vision, mission, and values of the nonprofit. Unless you keep these statements as the center of everything you do, you will be apt to flit from one thing to another and not be successful in any of them.

Challenges to Excellent Management

Besides the challenges of setting priorities and time management, there are three other major challenges every executive director faces:

- ◆ Limited resources

- ◆ Balancing the core elements of responsibility

- ◆ Internal controls

Excellent Management with Limited Resources

In my first nonprofit, there were a lot of volunteers involved. But I seemed to be spending most of my time trying to herd them around instead of doing what I knew I needed to do to achieve our vision and mission.

There were no written policies or procedures for managing the several hundred volunteers. The board of directors was committed to the mission, but I quickly discovered that most of them viewed me as an administrative assistant, not an executive director. And many of them felt it was their duty (every day) to tell me how to do my job.

The size of the nonprofit is not as much of a management issue as is the scale of the challenges. Particularly in smaller nonprofits, there is always a battle to find adequate resources to pay the executive director's salary, to fundraise, to administer programs, and to just keep the office running.

So how can you be excellent even when you have limited resources?

Budget

The number-one strategy for management excellence when the resources are limited is the annual board-

> The small, rural nonprofit was founded by the parents of the severely mentally and physically challenged clients. When the board of directors (composed of parents of clients) hired its first executive director, the members felt it was their duty to constantly monitor everything she did. Within six weeks, the executive director had a nervous breakdown. Every day, the parents and board members were at the building giving the executive director conflicting instructions on how to run the nonprofit. It was just too much for her to handle.

 stories from the real world

> In one nonprofit, the codirectors of the early-learning child care center funded by United Way had no idea how to put together a budget. The codirectors had helped start the center, which had been in operation for over a year before they admitted to the executive director of the United Way their lack of knowledge on how to develop a budget. They were functioning from day to day by operating to the limits of whatever money they had been able to raise. The United Way executive director was chagrined to discover she had not even bothered to ask the codirectors if they knew how to put a budget together.

 stories from the real world

approved budget. It is amazing how many nonprofits, especially those run without paid staff, do not have budgets. A good budget establishes the parameters within which you and the board operate. In other words, if it is not in the budget, eliminate it as a project or priority.

If like many nonprofit executive directors you have a social work background, you might never have taken an accounting course. Do not be afraid to admit you really don't know how to develop a budget. And if your board members have never been trained in budget development, it can be a case of the blind leading the blind.

If your nonprofit is operating without a budget, it will hinder your ability to grow and provide even more successful programs. You and your board must calculate what it is going to take in both income and expenses to carry out the mission. Plus, many foundations and other funders will not support an organization that does not have a budget.

A good budget is the road map for every facet of your responsibilities. Some basic steps to take in building a workable budget include the following:

◆ Chart the historical actual income and expenses. Evaluate how much money was raised (income) and how much money was spent (expenses) each year that your nonprofit has been in existence, and put the figures into a visual table using an Excel spreadsheet. If you do not know how to make a table from Excel, find a volunteer to help. There are also good accounting software packages that can help build and track a budget.

◆ Estimate income and expenses for one year. Based on the historical records of income and expense, estimate how much money needs to be raised for one year's operational expenses in each of the core elements, and then add 3 to 5 percent as a buffer for unexpected increases in costs.

◆ Get board approval for the budget. One of the board's governance responsibilities is fiscal oversight of the nonprofit, which is why the board must review and approve the annual budget. Establish a finance committee (a sample job description is included in **Chapter Two**), composed of board members and knowledgeable finance people (such as accountants and bankers), and they can actually develop the budget if you are not knowledgeable in budget development or in other financial management issues.

◆ Implement resource-development strategies based on the needs outlined in the budget. Once it is determined how

---

Base the budget on income and expenses for each of the core elements:

◆ *Administration*—office supplies, salaries and wages, benefits, insurance, travel expenses, meals, beverages for board and committee meetings, equipment, facility rental, utilities, and maintenance, etc.

◆ *Resource development*—expenses associated with raising money, the donor tracking software package

◆ *Marketing*—publicity, marketing materials, annual report, etc.

◆ *Programs*—supplies, equipment, insurance, etc.

◆ *Volunteer and board development*—recruitment, training, recognition, and dismissal strategies, database software for tracking volunteer information

◆ *Community involvement*—membership fees for senior staff in community organizations, such as Rotary, Kiwanis, Chamber, etc., as well as meals, entertainment, etc.

Example

much money is needed, fundraising strategies can be developed to bring in the necessary funds. *Caution: Never have more than 20 percent of the budget coming from any single source, because if that source dries up, the nonprofit will be in big financial trouble.*

◆ Establish policies and procedures to ensure solid, accountable financial management. The finance committee can develop financial management policies and procedures based on the standards of accounting for nonprofits as stated by the Financial Accounting Standards Board, which the board will need to approve (see **Chapter Three**).

Volunteers and Interns

Additional key resources for nonprofits are volunteers and interns. Even with limited financial resources, volunteers and interns can often make the difference between completing a project and not even starting on it. The vast majority of nonprofits were started by volunteers who had a passion around a specific issue or need. Many nonprofits function successfully for years as totally volunteer-driven organizations.

Sometimes, however, when the first executive director is hired, volunteers will pull back and reduce their level of involvement. "We have a staff person now," they say, "so I don't need to be as involved."

Nothing could be further from the truth. A savvy executive director knows that volunteers will always play a critical role in the nonprofit, as board members, committee members, and/or program volunteers. Interns can also provide valuable temporary assistance.

But volunteers don't always make your efforts for management excellence easy.

Nonprofits with limited staff are often confronted with the conflicting roles of volunteers. For example, a board member can also serve on a committee and be involved in the programs (e.g., mentoring clients, serving food at the soup kitchen, running fundraisers, etc.). Where conflict arises is when neither the board nor staff understands the lines of authority for each role or "hat" the volunteer is wearing.

It is for this reason that training on this issue is critical for all board, staff, and volunteers. The chart shows the various hats a board member can wear and where the lines of authority are for each volunteer and staff person. Use this chart in orientations of new board members, new staff, and anyone who volunteers for the nonprofit.

Make sure that the board has approved policies for the recruitment, training, recognition, and dismissal of all types of volunteers (chapters 1 and 6 of *Nonprofit Management Simplified: Board and Volunteer Development*). Where volunteers must play larger roles because of limited resources, such policies and procedures can be invaluable in increasing the management excellence of the nonprofit.

One of the most important staff positions for any nonprofit is that of volunteer coordinator. But even in large nonprofits, it is sometimes difficult to find a staff person whose sole responsibility is volunteer development. If you cannot afford a paid position for a volunteer coordinator, recruit a well-organized volunteer to do the job. Just make sure you give the volunteer a job description and monitor effectiveness with performance reviews, just like you would with a paid staff person.

Committees

Committees appointed by the board can be of tremendous help to you if you have limited resources. The chair and vice chair of the committees should always be board members, but add to the committee community volunteers with expertise in the specific responsibilities of the committee.

Having non-board members on the committees is a good training ground for potential board members. For example, the marketing committee should have volunteers on the committee who have experience and knowledge of marketing and branding issues (*Nonprofit Management Simplified: Board and Volunteer Development*). Following are some strategies that must be implemented for the committees to be excellent and productive.

Limit the Number of Committees

Regardless of the size of the nonprofit, there should generally be no more than six committees. Any more than that and the staff becomes too busy staffing the committees instead of doing its job. The organizational chart in **Chapter One** illustrates a committee structure based on the core elements. As your nonprofit grows, each of the three standing committees can be divided into two committees. If your nonprofit is totally volunteer driven with no paid staff, the suggested committee structure works very well too.

Develop Job Descriptions

Each committee should have a job description (chapter 1 of *Nonprofit Management Simplified: Board and Volunteer Development*) so committee members know exactly what their responsibilities are.

Train Committee Chairs

Committee chairs must be trained in how to be excellent meeting facilitators (chapter 3 of *Nonprofit Management Simplified: Board and Volunteer Development*) to avoid long, boring meetings that accomplish little. Remember, the mind can absorb only what the posterior can endure. And committee members and staff must frequently be reminded that the role of a committee is to advise, not to tell the staff what to do.

The founding executive director of a nonprofit serving developmentally delayed and physically challenged adults obviously had a passion for helping the clients learn employable skills. He was a social work graduate who had majored in vocational education. He knew his job well when it came to programs for the clients.

He had twenty staff members, but the turnover was high. He had to hire and train at least a third of the staff every two years. And one of the staff members who had been with the nonprofit the longest had just been arrested for abusing a client.

For the fifteen years the nonprofit had been in existence, the majority of its funding was provided by state and federal grants. But there were major cutbacks in funding to social services, and each month it became more and more difficult to generate enough income to cover expenses, let alone build a three- to six-month reserve. Now there was another similar program starting in the county that was run by a local church.

If that wasn't enough of a challenge for the executive director, the facility the nonprofit rented had just been sold, and there was only a month to find another location that would fit the budget.

The executive director was overwhelmed with competing stresses related to every aspect of the nonprofit. "I just want to help our clients," he told a peer. "All this other stuff is just detracting from our mission."

 stories from the real world

Excellent Management by Balancing the Core Elements

How do the sometimes-overwhelming negatives happen in a nonprofit? Is it a lack of funding that is the problem? Or is it possibly something else? Every executive director juggles a nonstop balancing act every day.

Ongoing strategic planning, judicious use of people, completion of projects, and paperwork must all be based on a constant effort to balance the time spent on each of the six core elements necessary for a nonprofit's success: administration, board/volunteer development, community involvement, resource development, marketing, and programs.

When you put too much emphasis and time on any one of the six elements while ignoring the other five, the wheels of the nonprofit begin to wobble. If you flit from one element to another and fail to manage the time you spend on each of the elements, chaos and disaster can creep up on you. The nonprofit may very well fail in its mission and go out of existence. So how can you bring balance to your efforts?

Administration

Let's face it. Some people are better at the administration of a nonprofit than others, which is why larger nonprofits often have several staff members covering all the various aspects of administration. But even with more staff, the executive director must periodically check to make sure all the proper policies and procedures are implemented in each of the key components of administration:

- ◆ Financial management (**Chapter Three**)—everything from bookkeeping to the way money is handled at a fundraising event

- ◆ Risk management (**Chapter Five**)—insurance, employee benefits, disaster preparedness and response, health and safety issues for staff and volunteers, abuse prevention, and crisis communication

- ◆ Human resources management (**Chapter Four**)—hiring, training, recognition, and dismissal of employees, including performance reviews and frequent reviews and updates of the employee handbook

- ◆ Facilities and equipment management (**Chapter Three** and **Chapter Five**)—rental or purchase of the facility and equipment, maintenance, and expansion issues

Board and Volunteer Development

Because of the critical role that volunteers play in every nonprofit, it is essential that you verify there are adequate policies and procedures related to the recruitment, training, recognition, and dismissal of all volunteers (chapters 1 and 6 of *Nonprofit Management Simplified: Board and Volunteer Development*): board members, committee members, and program volunteers.

Unfortunately, too often volunteers are *managed* rather than *developed*. If volunteers are regarded as critical resources for the nonprofit, monitoring and assessment of a formalized volunteer development program is a given, versus a dictatorial management approach that tells volunteers what to do, when, and where.

Board members especially should be fully trained on their governance roles and responsibilities (chapter 1 of *Nonprofit Management Simplified: Board and Volunteer Development*) to make sure the nonprofit meets or exceeds all legal requirements by local, county, state, and federal governments. And the excellent executive director will see board members as critical resources for advice on just about every aspect of management rather than as irritants to be placated or ignored.

One executive director told me, "I could get so much more done if it weren't for my board members meddling all the time."

Community Involvement

Because nonprofits operate for public benefit, there must be a board-approved plan to be constantly visible and involved within the community in which the nonprofit operates (*Nonprofit Management Simplified: Board and Volunteer Development*). Senior staff members need to be encouraged to join and become active in service organizations like Kiwanis, Rotary, Chamber of Commerce, etc. The dues for those organizations should be included in your annual budget. Such connections can prove extremely valuable, especially if specific funding needs arise.

Nonprofits must also be involved in or lead community collaborations around topics relevant to their missions. Collaboration is not only about sharing resources, but it is also about sharing knowledge and working together to address common issues.

What kind of reputation does your nonprofit have? Is the nonprofit regarded as the expert in a specific field? Is the nonprofit the one that government officials will approach when they are considering legislation specific to the nonprofit's mission?

A nonprofit had been in existence for more than twenty-five years. Its most expensive, time-consuming fundraiser was a rubber ducky race down the local river. People in the community would buy tickets, and each ticket included the number of a specific rubber duck. If a ticket number matched the number on the first duck to reach the finish line, the person holding the ticket would win a new car. Although the race had been held every year for ten years, the new executive director discovered several things:

◆ The high level of expenses associated with conducting the race meant that rarely did the nonprofit clear more than $2,000.

◆ The race was no longer known as the XYZ nonprofit's rubber ducky race, but simply the "Rubber Ducky Race," which meant the nonprofit was not even getting any marketing value from it.

◆ The staff was spending huge amounts of time preparing for and conducting the event when there were other things it could/should be doing.

◆ The board was unwilling to consider eliminating the race because it was a traditional community event.

 stories from the real world

The old fundraising adage "People give to people, not to organizations" is another key reason for you to be active within the community.

Resource Development

Fundraising is no longer just about raising funds but also about the development of all types of resources—short and long term—that will help the nonprofit achieve its mission. A variety of assessments will help you and the board understand which types of resource development strategies work and which need to be dropped.

The excellent nonprofit executive director will guide the board and the nonprofit into annual assessments of every resource-development strategy, comparing income with expenses (including the dollar value of staff and volunteer time) and developing resource development strategies that are the most cost effective while still providing marketing value.

But resource development isn't just about fundraising events. It is also about:

◆ The development of planned giving strategies that will have long-term financial benefit for the nonprofit

◆ Procurement of materials donated by local businesses, also known as gifts-in-kind

◆ Making sure that no more than 20 percent of the nonprofit's revenue comes from any single source to prevent major financial issues if that source is withdrawn

◆ Procuring enough resources so the nonprofit can establish a three- to six-month reserve fund

◆ Donor cultivation, donor recognition, database building of potential donors, donor thank-you, etc.

Marketing

Hopefully, you understand that publicity is not marketing. Publicity is only one of several strategies necessary to promote the brand, keep donors informed of successes, and build awareness of needs so that people, corporations, and foundations will make donations.

A major first step in building an effective marketing plan is the identification of the nonprofit's brand. Once the primary brand (or identity) of your nonprofit has been established, you can then develop a variety of marketing strategies based on the brand.

Never assume that just because the nonprofit generates a lot of brochures, has a website, publishes a newsletter, and publicizes events it is good at marketing. Good marketing is based on good market research.

Programs

Programs are all the strategies you use to meet the needs of identified clients. But programs that have been operating for years are not necessarily the valid approaches needed today to fulfill the mission. Just like each one of the other core elements, regular assessments and evaluations of the programs are critical.

The fast-paced change in the environment in which your nonprofit operates requires constant assessments. And more and more funders are looking for *outcomes* measurements versus *output* statistics. In other words, funders do not want to hear only about how many people were served but also about concrete examples or stories that show your programs made a difference in the lives of clients.

Donor fatigue, cutbacks in funding, and competition require you to establish research strategies that will collect data on the long-term impact of the programs on clients.

For example, it is not how many people were served food at the food bank but how many of those people now have jobs because the nonprofit also provided a job-training program for low-income and unemployed individuals.

The new executive director of a nonprofit with a $3 million budget and a staff of fifteen had the dubious pleasure of trying to follow in the footsteps of an executive director who was much loved and had been in the position for more than twenty years. Unfortunately, one of the first things the new director discovered was that the nonprofit was $1.2 million in debt, and the board did not know it.

How was the executive director going to convey the necessary financial-management issues to the board without denigrating the former director? How had the debt happened—and why? What needed to be done to prevent it from happening again?

stories from the real world

Excellent Management Based on Internal Controls

When the board has not approved policies that establish solid internal controls, the results can sometimes be devastating for a nonprofit, with malfeasance, embezzlement, and bad publicity causing every facet of the nonprofit to suffer. It is the excellent executive director's job to make sure the proper internal controls are implemented in every facet of the nonprofit.

This is an example that clearly illustrates what can happen when there is a lack of internal controls in every aspect of the nonprofit—but specifically in financial controls. And the lack of internal controls will eventually provide a huge drain on the executive director's time to correct the problems that will result.

Internal controls for any nonprofit include the following critical components:

Policies and Procedures

All board members and staff should have access to a constantly updated manual of board-approved policies and executive director-initiated procedures for each one of the core elements. **Appendix E** includes a checklist of the types of policies and procedures that should be included in a manual. **Appendix D** has some examples of policies.

Additional policies for all aspects of nonprofit management are included in all the chapters of these handbooks. It is easy to put the manual on a computer file with access limited to a password controlled site for authorized board members and staff. And only one or two people should be able to make changes to the manual. The manual must also be updated every time the board approves a new or changed policy.

Assessments

Sometimes nonprofits limit assessments to a strategic planning process. If you want to excel in your management strategies, you need to be constantly assessing every aspect of the core elements to make sure the board-approved policies and your implemented procedures are, in fact, being used. A variety of assessment tools is included in these books.

Place a check mark beside the assessments that you regularly do:

- ❑ I make sure there is adequate funding for every project or program.

- ❑ I know there are enough volunteers for every project or program.

- ❑ I know financial controls are being used by staff.

- ❑ I annually ask board members to verify that they are fulfilling their governance roles.

- ❑ I annually evaluate the adequacy of all insurance packages, including employee benefits.

- ❑ I have implemented disaster-preparedness strategies.

- ❑ My employees are involved in building a safe and healthy workplace.

- ❑ The supervisors of all staff and volunteers conduct annual performance reviews, with periodic updates between reviews or as needed.

Audits: Program and Financial

Regardless of the size of your nonprofit, periodic, unannounced audits of programs and financial management processes are essential. Board-level committee members can conduct these audits periodically just to make sure the policies they have approved are being used by staff and volunteers.

For example, the internal audit (**Chapter Three**) can be done by a member of the finance committee in the middle of the fiscal year just to verify that the right financial controls are in place and that the annual accounting audit will not reveal any procedural problems.

Remember, the monthly or quarterly treasurer's reports tell the board nothing about *how* the receipts and expenses are documented, so internal audits add an extra layer of accountability.

Training

Although training is often the last item added to a nonprofit's budget, it really should be given a greater priority. If staff and volunteers are not properly trained on internal controls, policies, and procedures—and there is no allowance for ongoing training—the nonprofit's capabilities for growth will be severely restricted.

Just like in the for-profit sector, the environment in which nonprofits operate is constantly changing. Staff and volunteers need to be always upgrading their knowledge and skills to know how to respond to those changes.

For example, social media and the Internet have had a profound impact on the way nonprofits market their programs and how they ask for funding. If your nonprofit staff does not know how to build a web page, interact on the Internet, and expand their sphere of influence through social media, you will lose out on tremendous opportunities.

Challenge yourself to keep your skills updated with new approaches via conferences and trainings. Executive coaching is one of the newest strategies for helping nonprofit executive directors focus on the areas where they are struggling. Be sure the coach has a lot of nonprofit experience as a CEO and make sure the board supports the coaching by allocating funds for it.

The best coaching results are achieved with a minimum of six months of sessions (once a month). Although the costs for coaching vary widely, expect to pay at least $100 an hour for a good coach. So six months of coaching for one hour a month would cost the nonprofit around $600. The coaching plan should include specific goals and expected outcomes, with the executive director doing some type of homework assignments between the sessions.

Time Management

Specific strategies of time management will help you balance how much time you spend on the people (volunteers and staff), projects (goal achievement and evaluation), and paperwork (the essential tools and research) for each of the core elements.

Executive Director Journal

The sample journal and executive director schedule are examples of two ways for you to track your schedule based on a hypothetical eight- to nine-hour day. This type of schedule groups projects, tasks, and core elements in one- to two-hour segments, while the journal groups tasks by the executive director core competencies and by the core elements.

Encourage other staff to develop similar time allotments to increase productivity and to ensure necessary goals, objectives, and action plans are completed promptly.

Sample Executive Director Journal

Date	Description	Time	Division: Admin, Fundraising, Specific Program	Organizational Objective or Core Competency
September 7	Staff meeting	1.5 hours	Admin	Provides effective staff leadership
	Board meeting preparation	1 hour	Admin	Provides leadership
	Phone calls to potential board members	1 hour	Admin	Relationship builder
	Attended Rotary meeting	1.5 hours	Admin	Skilled at community building and collaboration
	Reviewed donor database and prioritized potential leadership givers for contact by volunteers	2 hours	Fundraising	Skilled at resource development
	Met with staff accountant regarding the first audit; did internal audit; worked on financial policies to take to the finance committee	3 hours	Admin	Goal 1: Administration division; CPA does an audit Goal 2: Meet standards of accounting for nonprofits

Another way to look at time management is what is sometimes called the 80/20 rule: You get 80 percent of your results from 20 percent of your key tasks.

Veteran nonprofit consultant Ron Soto says: "The key is to determine what high-payoff activities or tasks will give you the greatest contribution to the priority core elements goals. Most managers get caught in the activity track, working on low-payoff activities."

By developing some time-management forms personalized to the manager's needs, it will be easier to track how time is spent as well as decide what are the most productive areas on which to focus. The chart illustrates some key issues that should be included on any manager's time-management forms. This is another example of a type of form that can easily be developed on an Excel spreadsheet.

Sample Executive Director Schedule

Time	Task	Core Element
8:00 to 10:00 a.m. (two hours for staff development)	Staff meetings and "walk around"	Administration, staff development
10:00 to 11:00 a.m. (one hour for board development)	Board telephone calls	Board/volunteer development
11:00 a.m. to noon (one hour on projects and paperwork)	Review mail and do updates on strategic plan	Administration/paperwork/projects

Time	Task	Core Element
Noon to 1:00 p.m. (one hour on cultivating potential donors)	Rotary	Community involvement
1:00 to 2:00 p.m. (one hour on projects and paperwork)	Work with accountant on annual budget	Administration/project/paperwork
2:00 to 3:00 p.m. (one hour on projects and paperwork)	Meet with internal operations director on policies and procedures manual	Administration/project/paperwork
3:00 to 4:00 p.m. (one hour on projects and paperwork)	Meet with marketing director and resource development director on annual fundraising appeal	Marketing, resource development/project/paperwork
4:00 to 5:00 p.m. (one hour on projects and paperwork)	Meet with board chair regarding next board meeting's agenda	Administration/project/paperwork

Executive Director Key Issues Form

At the beginning of each month, complete the form and indicate the priority level of each listed item. "A" means it is a must, or top priority. "B" indicates it needs to be done but could go to the next month. "C" indicates it will be done if there is time. Once the form for the month is completed, set up specific time slots during the day to work on the focus areas using a daily calendar divided into the eight-hour slots:

Sample Executive Director Priority Issues Form

Strategic Goals	Priority Level and Estimated Time Needed	People, Projects, or Paperwork Needed	Time Needed	Core Elements Covered
A three-year marketing plan will be developed that will increase brand identity by 30 percent.	B Eight hours, plus three one-hour focus groups	Interview marketing staff person; set marketing committee meeting; marketing assessment; Gary J. Stern's, "Marketing Workbook for Nonprofit Organizations, Volume I," Amherst H. Wilder Foundation, (ISBN 0-940-06901-6)	Two hours for committee meeting; four hours to interview, hire, and orient marketing person; two hours to complete workbook; three hours of marketing focus groups	Marketing administration volunteer development
A system of internal financial controls will be developed and implemented for testing by board members within one year.	A Twelve hours	Sample financial management policies/procedures and internal controls from the Hour Series	One hour for finance committee meeting; two hours/day to rewrite sample policies/procedures and internal controls	Administration

- ◆ Two hours a day on staff development

- ◆ One hour a day on volunteer development

- ◆ One hour a day on cultivating potential donors and volunteers

- ◆ Four hours a day on managing projects and paperwork related to strategic goals and the core elements

At the end of the month, put a check mark beside each task completed. Any tasks not completed should be transferred to the next month's forms. This form can really help executive directors keep track of how their time is spent.

Two Hours a Day on Staff Development

More staff decreases the issues related to limited resources, right? Wrong. Regardless of the number of staff, having paid personnel results in an additional set of management issues.

Regardless of the size or type of nonprofit, plan on spending at least two hours a day dealing with staff issues. This could include a weekly staff/team meeting, one-on-one meetings with staff for performance reviews, answering questions from a staff person related to a project being worked on, or referring staff to the relevant board-approved policies.

The leadership style of each executive director is different. I do not attempt to discuss here the importance of developing an effective leadership style but simply remind you how important it is to be constantly working on improving the strategies you use with staff.

There are some basic strategies you can use in your management and development of staff:

Establish Employee Policies and Procedures

Board-approved policies and procedures related to personnel management are critical if you are striving for excellence. You do not have to be an expert in human resources management, but at least take classes on your state's labor laws and on federal hiring and firing laws (see **Chapter Four**).

Too many executive directors make preventable mistakes in their hiring and firing that can cost the nonprofit thousands of dollars in wasted effort and

---

Here are some good organizing and time-management steps:

Monthly

- ◆ Establish a tracking system to measure goal completion.

- ◆ Give copies of your schedule to staff and volunteers who need to know your schedule.

- ◆ At the beginning or end of each month, review what was done the last month, and decide what needs to be carried over to the next month, what needs to be eliminated, what needs to be added or revised, and the priority of each.

- ◆ Compare your monthly goals with the critical strategic, personal, and professional goals.

Daily/Weekly

- ◆ Take time (five to ten minutes) at the beginning or end of each day to prioritize the day/week.

- ◆ Use the monthly calendar to organize your daily/weekly calendars.

- ◆ Estimate the amount of time you will need for each project, people, and paperwork, and block off that time accordingly.

- ◆ As each task/project is completed, check it off of the daily, weekly, and monthly calendars.

- ◆ Keep the calendars up to date!

- ◆ Use a computer-based system, such as Outlook or Access, and donor-management software to keep track of the projects, people, and paperwork.

Example

The executive director who had been in a single-staff nonprofit before now had to learn how to delegate to three other staff members instead of doing everything herself. The resource development director, or fundraiser, had also applied for the executive director position. When she didn't get it, she did her best to make the director's life miserable, challenging everything the director suggested.

The administrative staff person who was secretary, bookkeeper, and receptionist had a son who was dying and was, for obvious reasons, distracted and absent a lot. The third staff person, who was focused on programs, knew so little about leading a meeting that program committee meetings were mostly shouting matches between volunteers. And there was no way to measure the excellence of the programs other than how many people were helped.

The executive director developed personnel policies, with the help of a board committee. She met with the staff and asked for their help in addressing communication issues. Staff was also involved in the development of job descriptions for each position. As a result, the resource development director made the decision to leave, and a part-time person was hired to help the administrative staff person. The executive director worked with the program staff person and the committee chairs to learn how to conduct effective meetings. And when the board approved policies for program evaluations, the shouting matches at meetings were eliminated.

 **stories from the real world**

potential lawsuits. And a good policies and procedures manual for all the core elements that is available to all employees can often reduce the number of questions from staff that you will need to address.

Learn How to Manage Your Time

Often the more staff you have, the more pressures there are to interact and lead the staff. The excellent executive director, however, will learn how to manage time by implementing some essential strategies:

Keep a Journal or Date Book

Use a computerized or handwritten journal or date book to keep track of all appointments and projects. The journal can be a great resource to allocate time before and after a project starts. It also provides a visual record of how each day is spent so you are able to verify that time is being spent on strategic goals and on each of the core elements. Update the journal at the end of each day, transferring projects that did not get completed on to the next day's tasks. The journal is also a great resource for identifying how much time you are spending on specific grants or projects, which can be a big help to the accounting staff when it comes to allocating funds, especially if there are a variety of grants to programs.

Never assume that 100 percent of your time is spent on administration. Learn how to track your time by grants, fundraising, projects, or core elements. This will also help during the budgeting process to know what portion of your salary and benefits should be allocated to which category. This same strategy should be used by all administrative and senior staff who work across various divisions, programs, or grants.

Limit Interruptions

Limit staff interruptions to a specific time during the day or to only when you have your office door open. Train an administrative assistant to screen staff requests for help. In many instances, the assistant can refer the staff to the policies and procedures manual for answers to their questions.

Walk Through the Building

Walk around the building at least once a day. By doing this, you show you are interested in what every staff person is doing, plus the walking-around method of leadership will often help you identify issues needing your attention. For example, if you see that staff continually has problems with the copier, it alerts you to a potential repair expense, but it also identifies what could be a big stressor for staff who get frustrated when the copier is not working right.

Another strategy that works well is to not always use your office for meetings with staff. Take staff members to lunch, or meet in their offices. Staff can be intimidated when the executive director sits behind a desk all the time.

Prioritize Paperwork

Although it can be fun for you to open the mail to see which donors have sent checks, that task must and should be delegated to an administrative assistant or well-trained volunteer. Once the assistant has disbursed the mail, take your mail stack and immediately prioritize it into three categories:

- ◆ A = Must be dealt with today

- ◆ B = Can be put off for up to a week

- ◆ C = Optional items to be reviewed if there is time

If after a week, category C has not been touched, toss it into the wastepaper basket. Categories A and B should be stacked in priority order. Add to your calendar the projects, meetings, or paperwork—again, in priority order. Estimate the amount of time each project will take and enter it into a computerized journal or date book that has the day divided into thirty-minute slots. Just be sure that the computer journal is synced with your smartphone calendar.

There are a variety of ways to recognize staff achievements:

Thank-You Notes

Keep a supply of a variety of types of sticky notes available, and when you see a staff person going above and beyond, write something complimentary on the sticky note and place it on the employee's desk. Staff will be pleased that not only you noticed what they did but that you also took the time to say "thanks." It is easy to do these recognitions as you walk around the building. Keep a record of each person given appreciation notes, and make an effort to give at least one note to every employee during the year.

Salary, Wages, and Benefits

If you do not fight for increased payroll benefits, salaries, and wages for all staff during the annual budget-development process, who will? A good rule of thumb is for there not to be more than $10,000 difference in salary ranges for each management level. If, for example, the staff members find out that the director is making $100,000 or more and they are making minimum wage, it will not help to build good employee and management relationships.

Training and Professional Development

Be sure there is enough money in the budget for all staff to participate at least once a year in some type of training or professional development. If the budget is tight, use mini-staff retreats at the beginning or end of a workday for training. Again, if staff sees that management staff is traveling somewhere to attend conferences or trainings but there is no effort to develop lower-level employees' skills, it builds resentment and infers lack of fairness in how they are treated.

Example

Recognize Staff Achievements

Although the supervisor of each staff person should be responsible for the development of recognition strategies for outstanding performance, the executive director can also develop ways to provide unexpected recognitions.

Two Hours a Day on Volunteer Development

How can you deal effectively with the board? How do blatant power grabs occur in nonprofits? How do you deal with what I call, "mutant-ninja-turtle board members?" With these types of board members, I never knew when they were going to hide in their shell and not make a decision or when they were going to attack me like a ninja! Most nonprofit executive directors know exactly what I'm talking about.

However, I must make it clear that though it took me a while, I finally learned that board members can be one of the most valuable resources in my executive director tool kit. As my respect for board members' expertise increased, so did my willingness to access that expertise. My skills and knowledge are greatly expanded by the skills and caliber of board members.

The best donors are also volunteers. But that can lead to staff walking on eggshells when dealing with volunteers, afraid to confront problems for fear they will stop making contributions of time or money. Too few executive directors are willing to develop or implement policies that confront out-of-control or disruptive volunteers.

I learned the hard way that the best way to deal with disruptive volunteers was to ask key volunteers whom I trusted to meet with the difficult volunteer. A basic rule of thumb for communication with volunteers is "volunteer to volunteer." In other words, a volunteer may be more apt to listen to another volunteer than to a paid staff person. Plus, all volunteers (especially board members) must be carefully vetted to make sure they will fit with the nonprofit. Ask all volunteers to complete an application, and once they have been approved as volunteers, have them sign commitment-to-serve forms and give them job descriptions (chapters 2 and 6 of *Nonprofit Management Simplified: Board and Volunteer Development*).

The excellent executive director must be able to model for the rest of the staff the proper ways to deal with volunteers, regardless of whether or not they are board members, committee members, or program volunteers.

Although the board is responsible for the hiring and firing of the executive director, you must be involved in the development of board members through a board-level committee, such as a volunteer development committee.

Try to view committee volunteers as helpful resources for advice on specific facets of the nonprofit's management, rather than seeing them as just another group to tell you what to do. This viewpoint can greatly reduce the pressure on you to try to keep the committee members happy.

Program volunteers should be viewed as unpaid staff, even if they are board members. This view clearly demonstrates the need to develop policies and procedures that guide their recruitment, training, recognition, and dismissal.

Besides the implementation of volunteer development strategies, additional ideas for working with volunteers include:

Board Members

Keep a list of board members handy so that each day a short telephone call is made to at least one board member. The call could be simple: "Just called to see how you are doing." Or the call could be a list of specific questions:

- ◆ How do you think last week's board meeting went?

- ◆ Any suggestions on how you think we can have more effective meetings?

- ◆ What goals related to strategic planning do you think we need to spend more time on?

- ◆ What do you like or dislike about being on the board?

- ◆ How do you think we should handle XYZ issue?

Another strategy that works well for board development is for you to meet at least once a year with each board member. This can be done at lunch, breakfast, or some other one-on-one strategy where you and the board member get to know each other better. These kinds of meetings can also identify issues or problems before they show up at a board meeting or in your performance review.

Board retreats and trainings are another strategy that can be very effective for building a successful and cohesive board.

By the way, I always made it a point at the first meeting with each board member to say, "I urge you to always be completely open and honest with me, and I will grant you the same courtesy."

Committee Volunteers

Learning how to develop valuable board-level committees is critical, especially in a smaller nonprofit. By establishing committees that focus on each of the six core elements, you will have access to a wealth of information for decision-making, especially if the committee members are experts in their particular committees' responsibilities. Committees also become great training grounds for potential board members. Both you and the board members on the committees can observe the new committee members to see if they have the necessary skills for eventual board membership.

Just be sure that each committee has a job description so that the members know exactly what they are supposed to do. Remember, too, that committee members, like board members, must be trained in their roles, responsibilities, and lines of authority. Always look for ways to develop both staff and volunteers working on committees. Train committee chairs on how to conduct effective meetings (chapter 3 of *Nonprofit Management Simplified: Board and Volunteer Development*). Never assume that someone who is the head of a company necessarily knows how to run a meeting.

Program Volunteers

Although program volunteers will need to be recruited, trained, recognized, and dismissed (yes, volunteers can be dismissed) by their staff supervisors, the excellent executive director will make a special effort to know the volunteers by name and will always regard them as potential donors and board members. In smaller nonprofits where there may not be paid staff assigned to program volunteer supervision, other volunteers can be trained to serve as unpaid staff supervisors.

One Hour a Day Cultivating Potential Donors and Volunteers

Sometimes cultivating potential donors and volunteers can take years of effort by both the executive director and board members. But recruitment of their buy-in to the mission does not happen without planning and persistence. Remember, the number-one reason people say they do not give: "Nobody asked me to."

It is easy to become so busy with day-to-day tasks that cultivation strategies get lost in the shuffle. By scheduling time during the day to implement cultivation strategies, not only will you be more apt to enhance the volunteer development program, but you will be building the donor prospect list as well.

Suggestions for donor and volunteer cultivation strategies:

Database Management

The well-organized executive director will constantly be collecting information on potential donors and volunteers. Use specific donor database software or an Excel spreadsheet to keep track of these individuals, including notes on when they were contacted and by whom, as well as their responses.

There are lots of good donor-tracking software packages available that can help with this. Volunteers and other staff can also participate in this strategy. Regardless of how donors and volunteers are tracked, code them in some type of priority order: current givers and volunteers, high-net-worth individuals, community leaders, foundations, etc.

At one of the nonprofits where I worked, a board member mentioned that "George," a high-net-worth real estate developer in the area, had never made a donation. I sat down with a couple of board members who knew him, and we discussed what would be the best strategy to approach him and who should do it. I made the telephone call to introduce myself and ask if "Joe" (our board chair) and I could meet with him over lunch to talk about the critical health and human-care needs in the community. For the next four years, a variety of strategies were used with George. He and his wife were invited to fundraising events where community leaders were prevalent. They received invitations to join the nonprofit's prestigious leadership giving program, and sometimes a board member or I would just call to chat on the telephone.

Two years, later, George understood the mission of the nonprofit and willingly became a leadership giver, with contributions of over $10,000 a year. He even served a term as chair of the board.

stories from the real world

Telephone Calls

Sometimes a telephone call to simply introduce yourself and the nonprofit can be a segue into inviting the prospect to an event, scheduling a one-on-one meeting, or recruiting the employees of a company, for example, to volunteer for your nonprofit. When first using this strategy, track how long each call usually takes and arrange the daily schedule accordingly. For example, if each call takes about ten minutes, an estimated six calls can be made in one hour.

Honorary Chairs of Events

People give and volunteer for a variety of reasons, and sometimes community leaders and high-net-worth individuals like the recognition that comes with being named as the honorary chairs of specific events, such as annual golf tournaments.

Caution: Make sure that the honorary chair is given a job description that clearly outlines the responsibilities and the working relationship with staff in charge of the event. Otherwise, the executive director may end up with a power grab between the volunteer chair and the designated staff.

Membership in a Service Organization

There is a fundraising adage that says "People give to people, not to organizations." And it is very true. Keep this adage in the back of your mind as the basis for building relationships. A great way to do that

A talented young professional at a nonprofit was the staff person put in charge of the first golf tournament fundraiser. The honorary chair was never given a job description and made the wrong assumption that she was in charge of the event. When the staff person did not jump when she said "jump," the volunteer complained to the executive director and the staff person was fired. Obviously, in a case like this, neither the director nor the volunteer understood the proper lines of authority between volunteers and staff.

This story clearly illustrates the importance of communicating whether or not a volunteer's position is "honorary" or if the volunteer will be asked to do specific tasks under the leadership of the designated staff person.

stories from the real world

is to belong to a local service organization (Rotary, Kiwanis, etc.) where community leaders meet, greet, and serve the community.

The better the community leaders know you, the more apt they will be to give and volunteer for your nonprofit. Look for opportunities to speak at the meetings of service organizations. Most groups are always looking for speakers; however, they will usually not want the speech to be an appeal for funding but rather an overview of the issues confronting clients, success stories, or the history of the nonprofit.

Community Events

Excellent executive directors know that the more visible they are within their communities, the easier it will be to ask for contributions and for volunteers. Fit into the monthly or weekly schedule at least one community event. Everyone you meet is either a potential or current donor or volunteer.

Marketing Based on Brand Identity

Develop marketing strategies based on a board-approved identity for the nonprofit. Are you known in the community as the expert in a specific field of service? Is the nonprofit the first one people associate with a specific community need or issue?

Build your donor and volunteer cultivation strategies around the brand and marketing plan. Always carry with you brochures about your nonprofit. Be always alert to opportunities to speak about what the nonprofit does and how it is making a difference in the community.

Four Hours a Day Managing Projects and Paperwork

Whew! You are probably exhausted by this time: two hours working with staff, an hour working on volunteer issues, and an hour cultivating potential donors and volunteers. The day is half over, and your desk is full of projects and paperwork to complete.

By doing the people projects in the first half of the day, you will find that you will be reenergized to tackle the projects and paperwork in the last half of the day. People are the ones who fulfill the mission of any nonprofit. The more time you spend with the stakeholders of your nonprofit (staff, volunteers, donors, and clients), the greater the motivation will be for you to complete the projects and paperwork that provide the infrastructure for what those people do. Some executive directors would rather work on projects and paperwork in the morning and do the people development in the afternoon, or they alternate projects and people. Use whichever strategy works the best for you.

Managing projects requires many of the same strategies that are critical for people development:

Have a Plan

The board-approved document that should provide the basis for prioritizing projects is the strategic plan. If there is no strategic plan, make the development of one a priority project. A good strategic plan will include goals for each of the six core elements.

Obviously, there will be other staff and/or volunteers with responsibilities associated with the strategic plan, but you provide the leadership necessary to make sure the goals in the plan are accomplished.

One of the marketing goals might be: "A three-year marketing plan will be developed that will increase brand identity by 30 percent."

Your project related to the goal will be to meet with the marketing committee (unless your nonprofit is fortunate enough to have a marketing staff person) that begins the marketing process by identifying the brand of the nonprofit and developing a marketing plan.

Or one of the administration goals might be: "A system of internal financial controls will be developed and implemented for testing by board members within one year."

In this case, your project will be to meet with the auditor and staff accountant to develop a list of priority financial controls that can be tested before the end of the fiscal year by board members who are members of the finance committee.

Assign Responsibilities

Most projects are never solely the responsibility of the executive director; most require that volunteers and/or other staff complete some portion of the project.

For example, in the marketing goal, some responsibilities can be assigned to the marketing committee and/or the marketing staff person. It is your job to keep staff and volunteers on task to complete the project. Or, if there is no marketing staff person, you may have to take on some of the responsibilities that might ordinarily be assigned to staff. Better yet, assign the responsibilities to a qualified volunteer.

In the same way, the administration goal would include some responsibilities to be assigned to the auditor, the nonprofit's accountant, or a volunteer treasurer or committee.

Establish Timelines

If there are no target dates for completion of projects, nothing will be accomplished in a timely fashion. Part of your job is to juggle all the projects in such a way as to ensure their completion.

It does not mean that you have to do everything. Far from it! An excellent executive director has learned how to delegate but verify. Delegating responsibility does not mean you have no responsibility, but it means the responsibility is different: monitoring and leadership versus hands-on effort.

The marketing goals benchmarks might be:

◆ By March 1, marketing committee recommends a brand identity to the board.

◆ By June 1, a draft marketing plan is presented to the board for approval.

◆ By September 1, the marketing plan is implemented.

For the administration goal, short-term goals would be:

◆ By February 1, sample internal financial controls are collected from at least three other nonprofits.

◆ By April 1, finance committee has approved the internal financial controls.

◆ By May 1, policies related to financial controls are presented to the board for approval.

◆ By June 1, internal financial control policies are implemented, with policies entered into the policies manual.

◆ By September 1, internal audits are conducted to test implementation of the financial controls.

Example

Establish Benchmarks or Short-Term Goals

Rarely is a project completed in one sitting. Usually, there is a series of smaller projects that must be completed before the entire project is done or the goal accomplished.

In essence, managing projects and paperwork is all about organizational skills and strategies. If you do not feel you are very organized, learn how to be organized. Take a class, read a book on time management, or talk to people who are organized and get some tips from them. It is almost impossible to be an excellent manager without good organizational skills.

To Recap

- ◆ Make a conscious effort to balance all six of the core elements in the daily schedule.
- ◆ Verify that internal controls are implemented, especially for financial management.
- ◆ Incorporate time-management strategies.
- ◆ Spend quality time developing staff, volunteers (including board members), and donors.
- ◆ Allow time each day for managing projects and paperwork.

Appendix A—Sample Articles of Incorporation

(Should be reviewed by an attorney familiar with the law of tax-exempt organizations before filing with IRS)

Article I: Name/Registered Office

The name of this agency, a nonprofit corporation, shall be (*insert name*), hereinafter referred to as "nonprofit." The nonprofit's registered office is located at (*insert street address, zip code, and a mailing address*).

Article II: Purpose

This nonprofit is organized exclusively for charitable purposes within the meaning of Section 501(c)(3) of the Internal Revenue Code of 1986, as now enacted or hereafter amended, including, for such purposes, the making of distributions to organizations that also qualify as Section 501(c)(3) exempt organizations. To this end, the nonprofit shall (*enumerate specific purposes and activities*). All funds, whether income or principal, and whether acquired by gift or contribution or otherwise, shall be devoted to said purposes.

Article III: Limitations

At all times, the following shall operate as conditions restricting the operations and activities of the nonprofit:

- No part of the net earnings of the nonprofit shall inure to any member of the nonprofit not qualifying as exempt under Section 501(c)(3) of the Internal Revenue Code of 1986, as now enacted or hereafter amended, to any director or officer of the nonprofit, or to any other private persons, excepting solely such reasonable compensation that the nonprofit shall pay for services actually rendered to the nonprofit or allowed by the nonprofit as a reasonable allowance for authorized expenditures incurred on behalf of the nonprofit.

- No substantial part of the activities of the nonprofit shall constitute the carrying on of propaganda or otherwise attempting to influence legislation or any initiative or referendum before the public, and the nonprofit shall not participate in, or intervene in (including by publication or distribution of statements), any political campaign on behalf of, or in opposition to, any candidate for public office.

- Notwithstanding any other provision of these articles, the nonprofit shall not carry on any other activities not permitted to be carried on by a nonprofit exempt from federal income tax under Section 501(c)(3) of the Internal Revenue Code of 1986, as now enacted or hereafter amended.

◆ The nonprofit shall not lend any of its assets to any officer or director of this nonprofit (unless such loan program is regularly conducted as part of the activities of the organization and the qualification of the individual to participate in same is determined by a panel composed solely of non-board members) or guarantee to any person the payment of a loan by an officer or director of this nonprofit.

Article IV: Directors/Members

The nonprofit shall have a voting membership and may have classes of same (if any) as defined in the nonprofit's bylaws. The management and affairs of the nonprofit shall be at all times under the direction of a governing board of directors, whose operations in governing the nonprofit shall be defined by statute and by the nonprofit's bylaws. No member or director shall have any right, title, or interest in or to any property of the nonprofit.

The nonprofit's first board of directors shall be composed of the following natural persons: (*list directors' names and, optionally, addresses*).

Article V: Debt Obligations and Personal Liability

No member, officer, or director of this nonprofit shall be personally liable for the debts or obligations of this nonprofit of any nature whatsoever, nor shall any of the property of the members, officers, or directors be subject to the payment of the debts or obligations of this nonprofit.

Article VI: Dissolution

Upon the time of dissolution of the nonprofit, assets shall be distributed by the board of directors after paying or making provisions for the payment of all debts, obligations, liabilities, costs, and expenses of the nonprofit for one or more exempt purposes within the meaning of Section 501(c)(3) of the Internal Revenue Code, or the corresponding section of any future federal tax code, or shall be distributed to the federal government, or to a state or local government, for a public purpose.

Any such assets not so disposed of shall be disposed of by a court of competent jurisdiction of the county in which the principal office of the nonprofit is then located, exclusively for such purposes or to such organization or organizations as said court shall determine are organized and operated exclusively for such purposes.

Article VII: Incorporator

The incorporator(s) of this nonprofit is (are): (*insert names and addresses*).

The undersigned incorporator(s) certify both that she/he/they execute these articles for the purposes herein stated and that, by such execution, she/he/they affirm the understanding that should any of the information in these articles be intentionally or knowingly misstated, she/he/they are subject to the criminal penalties for perjury set forth in (*insert state*) statutes as if this document had been executed under oath.

Signatures:

Appendix B—Sample Bylaws

(Should be reviewed by an attorney familiar with the law of tax-exempt organizations)

Nonprofit:_____

Approved by the board of directors on: _____ (date)

Article I: Offices

Section One: Principal Office

The principal office of the corporation shall be located in the city of _____, county of _____, state of _____. The corporation may have such other offices, either within or without the state of _____, as the board of directors may determine or as the affairs of the corporation may require from time to time.

Section Two: Registered Office

The corporation shall have and continuously maintain in the state of _____ a registered office and a registered agent whose office is identical with such registered office as required by the state's Nonprofit Corporation Act. The registered office may be, but need not be, identical with the principal office in the state of _____, and the board of directors may change the address of the registered office from time to time.

Article II: Members

Section One: Members

Every individual who makes a financial contribution to the organization is classed as a member. The qualification, membership fees, and rights of a member shall (except as herein stated) be, as from time to time, determined by the board of directors.

Section Two: Voting Rights

Each member shall be entitled to one vote on each matter submitted to a vote of the members.

Section Three: Resignation

Any member may resign by filing a written resignation with the secretary, but such resignation shall not relieve the member so resigning of the obligation to pay any dues, assessments, or other charges theretofore accrued and unpaid.

Section Four: Transfer of Membership

Membership in this corporation is not transferable or assignable.

Article III: Meetings of Members

Section One: Annual Meeting

An annual meeting of the members shall be held during the first three months of each fiscal year for the purpose of electing directors, publication of the written annual report, and the transaction of other business as may come before the meeting. The day and time of such annual meeting shall be as determined by the board of directors. In the absence of such action by the full board of directors, the executive committee is so empowered. If the election of directors shall not be held on the day designated herein for any annual meeting, or at any adjournment thereof, the board of directors shall cause the election to be held as soon as thereafter convenient.

Section Two: Special Meetings

Special meetings of the members may be called by the chair of the board, the president, the board of directors, or not less than one-tenth of the members having voting rights.

Section Three: Place and Time of Meeting

The place and time for each meeting of members shall be designated by the board of directors or other person(s) calling same, which shall be reasonably convenient. If no designation is made, the place of the meeting shall be the registered office of the corporation in the state of _____, and the time for the meeting shall be 12:01 p.m.

Section Four: Notice of Meeting

Written, emailed, or printed notice stating the place, day, and hour of any meeting of members shall be delivered, either personally, electronically, or by mail, to each member entitled to vote at such meeting not less than ten or more than fifty days before the date of such meeting, by or at the direction of the chair of the board, or the secretary, or the persons calling the meeting. In case of a special meeting or when required by statute or these bylaws, the purpose or purposes for which the meeting is called shall be stated in the notice. If mailed, the notice of the meeting shall be deemed to be delivered one day after mailed if deposited in the US Mail addressed to the member at the member's address as it appears on the records of this corporation, with postage thereon prepaid.

Section Five: Quorum

Those members present at any meeting shall constitute a quorum.

Section Six: Proxies

No member may vote by proxy or agent in cases of election of directors by cumulative vote.

Article IV: Board of Directors

Section One: General Powers

Its board of directors shall manage the affairs of the corporation. Directors shall be residents of the state of _____. Directors shall serve on at least one management division committee or shall be officers of the corporation.

Section Two: Number, Tenure

Subject to the provisions of the following sentences, the number of directors shall be no fewer than eleven and no more than twenty-five, and each shall hold office until the second annual meeting of members following the director's election or until the director's successor be elected (whichever is later). Directors may serve a maximum of three consecutive two-year terms before rotating off the board of directors for not less than one year before they become eligible for additional service on the board of directors.

Effective _____, current directors whose tenure exceeds four consecutive years of service on the board may complete their current term plus one additional two-year term. The limiting of service on the board to three consecutive two-year terms before succession shall not have the effect of preventing a director from serving as an officer-elect or an officer past the three-term period for the purpose of completing the term of office or office-elect or successive office.

Section Three: Meetings

An annual meeting of the board of directors shall be held without notice immediately before or after, and at the same place as, the annual meeting of members. The board of directors may provide by resolution the time and place, either within or without the state of _____, for the holding of additional regular meetings of the board.

Regular meetings of the board of directors shall be held no less than four times a year at such times and places as the board of directors may fix by resolutions. In the absence of such action by the full board of directors, the executive committee is empowered.

Section Four: Special Meetings

Special meetings of the board of directors may be called by the chair of the board, the president, or not less than one-fourth of the directors. The officer or directors calling the special meeting shall designate the place and time therefore, which shall be reasonably convenient. If no designation is made, the place of the meeting shall be the registered office of the corporation, and the time for the meeting shall be 12:01 p.m.

Section Five: Notice of Meetings

Written, emailed, or oral notice stating the place, date, and hour of any regular or special meeting of the board of directors shall be delivered personally, by telephone, electronically, or by mail to each director entitled to vote at such meeting not less than twenty-four hours prior to the hour of such meeting by or at the direction of the officer or directors calling same.

If mailed, the notice of a meeting shall be deemed to be delivered one day after mailed if deposited in the US Mail addressed to the director at the address as it appears on the records of the corporation, with postage thereon prepaid. Neither the business to be transacted at nor the purpose of any regular or special meeting of the board of directors need be specified in the notice.

Section Six: Waiver

Any director may waive notice of any meeting. The attendance of a director at any meeting shall constitute a waiver of notice of such meeting, except where a director attends a meeting for the express purpose of objecting to the transaction of any business because the meeting is not lawfully called or convened.

Section Seven: Quorum

One-third of the board of directors shall constitute a quorum for the transaction of business at any meeting of the board of directors.

Section Eight: Manner of Acting

The act of a majority of the directors present at a meeting at which a quorum is present shall be the act of the board of directors unless the act of a greater number is required by law or by these bylaws. The board of directors shall keep regular minutes of its proceedings.

Section Nine: Vacancies

Any vacancies occurring on the board of directors shall be filled by a majority of the remaining directors though less than a quorum of the board of directors. A director elected to fill a vacancy shall be elected for the unexpired term of the predecessor in office.

Section Ten: Qualification

A majority of the board of directors shall be volunteers who are not members or staff of other agencies' boards. In case of dispute as to the qualification of a person, the decision of the board of directors shall be final and conclusive.

Section Eleven: Removal

The failure of any directors to attend at least two consecutive meetings of the board of directors without an excuse acceptable to a majority of the board shall constitute good cause for removal, and such absent director may be removed automatically from membership as a director of the corporation without the necessity of further action.

Section Twelve: Proxy

No director may vote by proxy or agent.

Section Thirteen: Nominations

A nominating committee will be appointed annually by the board of directors to fill any director vacancies, whether from expiration of terms or resignation. The nominating committee will be composed of a majority of members of the board of directors. Total membership on the committee shall be no more than ten and no fewer than five.

Article V: Officers

Section One: Officers

The officers of the corporation shall be a chair of the board, committee chairs and vice chairs, a secretary, a treasurer, an assistant treasurer, the immediate past chair of the board, and such other officers as may be elected in accordance with the provisions of this Article and Article X.

The board of directors may elect or appoint such other officers, including more assistant secretaries and more assistant treasurers as it shall deem desirable, such officers having the authority to perform the duties prescribed from time to time by the board of directors. No one person may hold two offices, nor shall any person hold the same office in this corporation for more than two consecutive terms.

Section Two: Election and Term of Office

The officers of this corporation shall be elected by the board of directors from the membership thereof at the annual meeting of the board of directors, and each officer shall hold office for one year from such date or until the officer's successor is elected, whichever is later. A nominating committee, as stated in Article IV, Section Thirteen, shall select and recommend officers to the board of directors for election at the annual meeting of the corporation.

Section Three: Removal

Any officer elected or appointed by the board of directors may be removed by the board of directors whenever, in its judgment, the best interest of the corporation would be served thereby, but such removal shall be without prejudice to the contract rights, if any, of the officer so removed.

Section Four: Vacancies

A vacancy in any office because of death, resignation, removal, disqualification, or otherwise may be filled by the board of directors for the unexpired portion of the term.

Section Five: Chair of the Board

The chair of the board shall be the principal officer of the corporation. The chair shall preside at all meetings of the members and of the board of directors. The chair may sign, with the secretary or any other proper officer of the corporation authorized by the board of directors, any deeds, mortgages, contracts, or other instruments that the board of directors has authorized to be executed, except in cases where the signing and execution thereof shall be expressly delegated by the board of directors, or by these bylaws, or be granted by statute to some other officer or agent of the corporation; and, in general, the chair shall perform all duties incident to the office of chair of the board and such other duties as may be prescribed by the board of directors from time to time.

Section Six: Vice Chair of the Board

In the absence of the chair of the board or in the event of the chair's inability or refusal to act, one of the committee or division chairs shall be selected to serve as vice chair of the board and shall be appointed to perform the duties of chair of the board, and when so acting, shall have all the powers of and be subject to all the restrictions upon the chair of the board. The vice chairs of the board shall perform such other duties as from time to time may be assigned to them by the chair of the board or by the board of directors.

Section Seven: Treasurer

The treasurer shall have or cause to have someone in charge of and custody of and be responsible for all funds and securities of the corporation, receive and give receipts for monies due and payable to the corporation from any source whatsoever, deposit all such monies in the name of the corporation in such banks, trust companies, or other depositories as shall be selected in accordance with the provisions of Article XI, Section Three of these bylaws and, in general, perform all the duties incident to the office of treasurer and such other duties as from time to time may be assigned to him/her by the chair of the board or by the board of directors.

Section Eight: Secretary

The secretary shall keep or cause to be kept the minutes of the meetings of the members and minutes of the meeting of the board of directors in one or more books provided for that purpose; see that all notices are duly given in accordance with the provisions of these bylaws or as required by law; be custodian of the corporate records and of the seal of the corporation and affix the seal of the corporation to all documents, the execution of which on behalf of the corporation under its seal is duly authorized in accordance with the provisions of these bylaws; keep a register of the post office address of each member, director, and officer of the corporation, which shall be furnished by the secretary to any director or officer; and in general, perform all duties incident to the office of secretary, and such other duties as from time to time be assigned to the secretary by the chair of the board or board of directors.

Section Nine: Assistant Treasurer

In the absence of the treasurer, or in the event of the treasurer's inability or refusal to act, the assistant treasurer shall perform the duties of the treasurer and, when so acting, shall have all the powers of and be subject to all the restrictions upon the treasurer. Such assistant treasurer shall perform such other duties as from time to time may be assigned by the chair of the board or by the board of directors.

Section Eleven: Other Officers

Committee or division chairs and vice chairs shall act as facilitators of committee meetings and perform such other duties as from time to time may be assigned by the board. Other officers, if any, shall perform such duties as shall be assigned to them by the chair of the board or the board of directors.

Article VI: Executive Committee

Section One: Constituency

The number of executive committee members shall be at least five, to include the officers of this corporation: chair of the board, the committee chairs and vice chairs, secretary, treasurer, assistant treasurer, and the immediate past chair of the board.

Section Two: Authority

Between meetings of the board of directors, the executive committee shall have and exercise the authority of the board of directors in the management of this corporation. All actions of the executive committee shall be consistent with policies adopted by the board of directors and shall be reported at the next meeting of the board of directors. The designation and appointment of any such committee and the delegation thereto of authority shall not operate to relieve the board of directors or any individual director of any responsibility imposed on the board or director by law.

Section Three: Vacancies

Any vacancies on the executive committee shall be automatically filled by the election of the officer by the board of directors and shall herein be constituted as a member of the executive committee.

Section Four: Tenure and Qualifications

Each member of the executive committee who is so enrolled by virtue of being an officer or designated member shall hold such membership coextensive with that member's tenure in such office.

Section Five: Meetings

Meetings of the executive committee may be called by the chair of the board, the president, or not less than one-fourth of the membership thereof. The officers or members authorized to call such meeting may fix the time and place of said meeting, which shall be reasonably convenient, but if no designation of the place of the meeting is made, the place of meeting shall be the registered office of the corporation in the state of _____, and the time for such meeting shall be 12:01 p.m.

Section Six: Notice

Written, electronic, or oral notice stating the place, date, and hour of any meeting of the executive committee shall be delivered personally, electronically, by telephone, or by mail to each member of the committee not less than twenty-four hours prior to the hour of such meeting by or at the direction of the officer or the members calling same. If mailed, the notice of a meeting shall be deemed to be delivered one day after mailed if deposited in the US Mail addressed to the member at the member's address as it appears on the records of the corporation, with postage thereon prepaid. Neither the business to be transacted nor the purpose of any meeting of the executive committee need be specified in the notice of such meeting.

Section Seven: Waiver

Any member of the executive committee may waive notice of any meeting. The attendance of a member at any meeting shall constitute a waiver of notice of such meeting, except where a member attends a meeting for the express purpose of objecting to the transaction of any business because the meeting is not lawfully called or convened.

Section Eight: Quorum

One-third of the members of the executive committee shall constitute a quorum for the transaction of business at any meeting thereof, and the act of a majority of the members present at a meeting at which a quorum is present shall be the act of the executive committee.

Section Nine: Prohibited Actions

Irrespective of the general powers delegated to the executive committee under Article VI, Section Two, said executive committee shall not have the authority of the board of directors with reference to amending the articles of incorporation; adopting a plan or merger or adopting a plan of consolidation with another corporation; authorizing the sale, lease, or exchange of all or substantially all the property and assets of the corporation; authorizing the voluntary dissolution of the corporation or revoking proceedings therefore; adopting a plan for the distribution of the assets of the corporation; or amending, altering, or repealing any resolution of the board of directors which by its terms provides that it shall not be amended, altered, or repealed by such committee. This section and the prohibitions herein stated shall be deemed paramount and superior to all other provisions of these bylaws.

Section Ten: Electronic Meeting

Subject to the provisions for notice required by these bylaws, the executive committee may participate in and hold a meeting by means of telephone conference, videoconferencing, or similar communications equipment by which all persons participating in the meeting can hear each other. Participation in the meeting shall constitute presence in person at the meeting, except when a person participates in the meeting for the express purpose of objecting to the transaction of any business on the ground that the meeting is not lawfully called or convened.

Section Eleven: Procedure

The executive committee may fix its own rules of procedure that shall not be inconsistent with these bylaws and shall keep regular minutes of its proceedings. Minutes of meetings shall be given to the board of directors for its review within thirty days of a meeting. Only the minutes of closed meetings (such as the executive director's performance review) need not be shared with the board of directors and will be marked and kept as "confidential" unless otherwise requested by the board of directors in writing and as a result of a vote of approval for the action by the board.

Article VII: Committees

Section One: Committees of the Board of Directors

In addition to the executive committee provided herein, the board of directors by resolution or appointment may designate one or more committees, each of which shall consist of two or more directors, which committees, to the extent provided in said resolution, shall act as advisors to the board and staff on designated issues; subject, however, to the prohibitions contained in Article VI, Section Nine, of these bylaws. The designation and appointment of any such committee and the delegation thereto of authority shall not operate to relieve the board of directors or any individual director of any responsibility imposed by law. Suggested committees include administration, resource development, marketing, programs, community involvement, board/volunteer development committee.

Section Two: Membership

Individual members of the community who are not board members may serve on the committees. Staff may be designated by the executive director to serve on committees.

Section Three: Chairs and Vice Chairs

The chair and vice chair of any board-appointed committee must be a member of the board of directors.

Article VIII: Executive Director

Section One: Executive Director

The board of directors may, at its option, employ an executive director who will serve as a nonvoting ex officio member of the board of directors.

Section Two: Term

The executive director shall serve for as long as the board of directors, by contract or otherwise, shall employ the executive director.

Section Three: Duties

The executive director shall supervise and direct the operation of the business of this corporation, the personnel employed thereby, and the public relations with respect thereto. The precise services of the aforesaid may be extended, curtailed, and/or further defined, from time to time, at the direction of the board of directors.

Section Four: Supervision

The supervisor of the executive director shall be the chair of the board, subject to the direction and authority of the board of directors. The annual evaluation of the executive director's performance shall be conducted by the executive committee and shall be based solely on the job description and previously agreed-upon job objectives.

Article IX: Contracts, Checks, Deposits, and Funds

Section One: Contracts

The board of directors may authorize any officer or officers, agent or agents of the corporation, in addition to the officers so authorized by these bylaws, to enter into any contract or to execute and deliver any instrument in the name of and on behalf of the corporation, and such authority may be general or confined to specific instances.

Section Two: Checks, Drafts, Etc.

All checks, drafts, or order for payment of money, notes, or other evidence of indebtedness issued in the name of the corporation, shall be signed by such officer or officers, agent or agents of the corporation in such a manner as shall from time to time be determined by resolution of the board of directors. Such instruments shall be signed by two of the following: treasurer, assistant treasurer, chair of the board, committee chairs of the board, executive director or other board member so designated by the board of directors. Two signatures are not needed for checks issued in amounts under $5,000.

Section Three: Deposits

All funds of the corporation shall be deposited from time to time to the credit of the corporation in such banks, trust companies, or other depositories as the board of directors may select.

Section Four: Gifts

The board of directors may accept on behalf of the corporation any contribution, gift, bequest, or device for the general purposes or for any special purpose of the corporation.

Article X: Books and Records

The corporation shall keep correct and complete books and records of account in compliance with the laws of the state of _____, including, but not limited to, the state Nonprofit Corporations Act; shall keep minutes of the proceedings of its members, board of directors, executive committee, and any other committee having authority of its board of directors; and shall keep at the registered or principal office a record giving the names and addresses of the members entitled to vote and of the directors and officers. Any member entitled to vote or any director or director's agent or attorney may inspect all books and records of the corporation for any proper purpose at any reasonable time.

Article XI: Fiscal Year

The fiscal year of the corporation shall begin on the first day of January and end on the thirty-first day of December of each year.

Article XII: Seal

The board of directors shall provide a corporate seal, which shall be in the form of a circle and shall have inscribed thereon the name of the corporation and the words "corporate seal." The use of such seal on a document is not required to make it legally binding on the corporation.

Article XIII: Nondiscrimination

Members, directors, officers, employees, agents, and clients of this corporation shall be selected without discrimination by reason of race, color, religion, sex, marital status, national origin, age, or handicapping condition.

Article XIV: Amendment

The power to alter, amend, or repeal these bylaws is delegated to the board of directors, and these bylaws may be amended at any annual, regular, or special meeting of the board of directors by a majority vote of the directors present, provided a quorum is present, and provided at least thirty days' notice of the proposed amendment has been given to each director at the direction of the chair of the board or if a special meeting, the officer, or director calling same.

Article XV: Special Provisions

No part of the net earnings of this corporation shall inure to the benefit of any individual. The property of this corporation is irrevocably dedicated to charitable purposes, and upon liquidation, dissolution, or abandonment of the owner, after providing for the debts and obligations thereof, the remaining assets will not inure to the benefit of any private person, but will be distributed to a nonprofit fund, foundation, or corporation that is organized and operated exclusively for charitable purposes and has established its tax-exempt status under Section 501(c)(3) and 509(a)(1), (2), or (3) of the Internal Revenue Code of 1954.

Appendix C—Core Elements Assessment

Board and staff members should place a check mark beside each standard they know the nonprofit meets or exceeds. Return only the last page to _____ by the deadline indicated in the cover letter. Be sure your name is on the last page before sending to the consultant or ED so your copy can be returned to you after tallying.

Standards/Benchmarks

✓	I. Basic Infrastructure
	A. Vision/Mission/Values
	1. The organization has a board-approved vision statement.
	2. The vision statement is no more than twenty-five words, contains no action words but states the ideal, ultimate goal of the organization. It answers the question, "Why does the organization exist?"
	3. The vision statement is reviewed by the board and staff at least every other year.
	4. The organization has a board-approved mission statement.
	5. The mission statement is short (twenty-five words or fewer), concise and clearly understood.
	6. The mission statement includes action words that answer the question, "What will the nonprofit do to achieve the vision?"
	7. The current programs of the nonprofit accurately reflect the mission statement.
	8. The mission statement is reviewed by the board and staff at least every other year.
	9. The nonprofit has a board-approved values or ethics statement included in relevant marketing materials and is posted in the organization's facilities.

B. Organizational Structure
1. An organizational chart shows a workable relationship between staff, volunteers, the board of directors, and board committees.
2. The board committees include oversight of all of the core elements: administration, board/volunteer development, resource development, marketing, programs, community involvement.
3. The organization is, or is under the management of, an organization incorporated and exempt from federal income tax (under the provision of Section 501(c) of the Internal Revenue Code) and has complied with all state and local codes.

C. Strategic Planning
1. The nonprofit annually examines internal trends, community trends, and national trends (social, philanthropic, political, and economic) to plan for the future.
2. The board annually develops realistic short- and long-range goals consistent with the organization's vision, mission, and values and which encompass all aspects of the organization.
3. There are written, measurable objectives and time frames for achieving them.
4. Implementation of the objectives is assigned to specific staff, volunteers, and/or committees.
5. The organization at least annually evaluates its programs, based on objectives, work plans, and outcome measures.
6. The board periodically plans and conducts a management audit of all internal and external operations, including the operations of the board and incorporates the audit into the planning process.
7. A variety of evaluation and assessment strategies are included in the organization's planning process and include identification of deficiencies and recommendations for correcting them.
8. Board members, staff, volunteers, and community stakeholders participate in the annual review and evaluation of the organization.
9. Total quality management is a board-approved operational procedure and philosophy, which is incorporated into the strategic plan.
10. The primary customer of the organization has been identified and ways to provide and measure top quality customer service have been implemented.

✓	II. Core Element—Administration
	A. Policies and procedures
	1. All legal documents are easily accessible when needed by staff or volunteers.
	2. A document checklist indicates the location of all legal documents.
	3. A policies and procedures manual is available for all staff and board members.
	4. The policies and procedures manual is updated at least annually.
	B. Financial
	1. The board has assigned financial oversight to a board standing committee, which presents easily understandable, written financial reports to the board at least quarterly.
	2. At least two signatures are required on all checks over a designated amount.
	3. Consecutive, numbered receipts are given out with all cash contributions.
	4. The annual budget is developed by staff, presented to the Finance Committee, approved by the board.
	5. Treasurer's reports include balance sheets.
	6. Treasurer's reports include amounts budgeted, amounts received and expended, and the variances, both monthly (or quarterly) and year-to-date.
	7. The board regularly evaluates its investment and banking policies to ensure the best possible management of the organization's funds.
	8. A certified audit is performed annually by an independent auditor (If the annual budget is below $100,000, a financial review is acceptable).
	9. The annual audit is unqualified, or if qualified, a plan to resolve the problems is presented to the board by the ED.
	10. A management letter from the CPA is provided and includes suggestions for improvements in the Internal Management of the nonprofit.
	11. The auditor includes a review of the accounting system in the yearly audit.
	12. The accounting books or computerized system are easily accessible to the board and are located in the organization's office in a secure location.
	13. Backup copies of computerized financial information are kept off-site or on the Internet Cloud.

	14. Required legal documents (e.g., IRS 990, W-2, etc.) are filed each year.
	15. The accounting system adheres to the basic standards of accounting for nonprofits.
	16. The organization has or is working toward accumulating a positive fund balance, including a six-month operating reserve.
	17. Fund accounting methods assure clear delineation of each grant's income and expenses, with no interfund borrowing.
	18. The accounting system includes methods for showing income and expenses for all of the core elements and for each program.
	19. All staff is trained on how to track their time so as to distinguish between administrative, program, and fundraising expenses.
	20. Accounting staff is trained on how to divide expenses, especially salaries and benefits, between administrative, program, and fundraising expenses, based on staff time records.
	C. Human Resources (Personnel)
	1. Personnel policies are maintained and evaluated regularly and are verified in compliance with state and federal employment laws.
	2. Personnel files are maintained on all staff in a secure location.
	3. Personnel files are accessible only to designated supervisors, the employee (with a supervisor present), and designated board members.
	4. All staff, except the ED, is annually reviewed and evaluated by the ED or the designated supervisor.
	5. The stability and consistency of management staff are demonstrated by low turnover.
	6. Written job descriptions and wage/salary ranges are available for all staff.
	7. If there is no paid staff, job descriptions and board expectations of volunteers are written and agreed upon.
	8. If there is no paid staff, evaluations of administrative volunteers are done by board members, based on written expectations, policies, and procedures.
	9. The administrative budget includes funds for staff and volunteer training and professional development.

	10. The organization has a written affirmative action policy that clearly states it will operate without discrimination in the selection of board members, volunteers, committee members and in the employment of staff in all protected classes, such as age, sex, ethnicity, religion, and sexual orientation.
	11. A formal process is established and followed for the annual review or evaluation of the ED by the board.
	D. Facilities & Equipment
	1. Facilities and equipment are maintained in a neat and orderly manner.
	2. Facilities and equipment are appropriate to the mission.
	3. Facilities, equipment, and overall atmosphere contribute to staff and volunteer safety, enthusiasm, and production and are ergonomically correct and handicapped accessible when required by law.
	4. The board has a policy for procurement, maintenance, and replacement of equipment.
	E. Risk Management
	1. Employee benefits include unlimited major medical, disability, and life insurance.
	2. An employee or volunteer committee annually evaluates health and safety issues related to the facility, the grounds, and equipment that can negatively impact employees, staff, volunteers, clients, etc.
	3. The nonprofit has internal and external disaster plans; volunteers and staff are trained how to respond.
	4. Directors and officers liability insurance is included in the budget.
	5. General liability insurance for staff and volunteers is adequate to meet the risks of the programs.
	6. The state's Good Samaritan laws are annually reviewed to verify compliance by the nonprofit.
	7. Policies and procedures clearly outline prevention and response strategies for all risky behavior by staff, volunteers, clients, or the public, such as sexual harassment, domestic violence, substance abuse, client abuse, etc.
	8. Property insurance is included in the budget.
	9. The board at least annually evaluates whether time, crime, automobile, or other insurance is needed.
	10. Workers compensation insurance is included in the budget.
	11. Crisis communication policies state who speaks for the organization, when they speak, and the process for developing statements to the press.

✓	III. Core Element—Board and Volunteer Development
	A. Board of Directors
	1. The board of directors has a minimum of ten active members.
	2. When multiple geographical areas are served by the nonprofit, volunteer advisory boards are established with clear lines of communication to the board of directors.
	3. The board of directors meets at least quarterly.
	4. At least 50 percent of the board members regularly attend all board meetings.
	5. Terms of office for the board of directors are clearly stated in the bylaws with no board member allowed to serve more than two consecutive terms.
	6. No more than one staff person (the ED) serves as an ex officio, nonvoting board member, and the ED does not serve as chair of the board.
	7. Agendas are prepared and mailed ahead of time for board and committee meetings, with input from the committee chair and the designated staff person.
	8. Standing committees meet regularly and report to the full board at each meeting.
	9. Minutes of all board and executive committee meetings are kept in an easily accessible location, with the minutes of the previous meeting available at each meeting.
	10. Board members are trained in their roles, responsibilities, lines of authority (in relationship to staff), and on how to conduct effective meetings.
	11. At the beginning of each term, board members sign a commitment-to-serve, confidentiality, and conflict-of-interest statements.
	12. Succession plans are in place for all officers of the board.
	B. Volunteer Development
	1. The nonprofit has written, board-approved policies for the recruitment, training, recognition, and dismissal of all volunteers: board, committee, and program.
	2. All volunteers and staff understand their roles and responsibilities, including legal and personal liabilities, and lines of authority.
	3. The demographics of all volunteers reflect the communities served.
	4. Job descriptions are available for all volunteer positions.

	5. A board-level committee is responsible for oversight of the volunteer development policies and procedures for all volunteers, including nominations of board members and officers.
✓	**IV. Core Element—Programs**
	1. The services/programs of the nonprofit adhere to the mission statement.
	2. All services/programs are provided without bias and in a nonpartisan manner.
	3. Political and religious activities are avoided, except to the extent allowed by law.
	4. Cooperative efforts with other nonprofits are evident.
	5. The organization has an ongoing process for examining and adapting programs to changing customer/client and community needs.
	6. No program is started until a plan has been presented to the board that includes why the program is needed, how it will be implemented, the resources needed, the expected length of the program, and evaluation and outcomes measurements methods for program effectiveness.
	7. Distribution of funds to programs and strategies are periodically examined for possible updating or improvement.
	8. Resource and needs assessments are used in the development of program priorities.
	9. All programs are evaluated at least annually, using predetermined indicators and outcomes measurements, with the results of the evaluations presented first to the board-level program committee and then to the board.
	V. Core Element—Community Involvement
	1. The staff is encouraged to be involved with community organizations to increase awareness of the nonprofit and its programs and to better understand other programs and services available to their customers/clients.
	2. The nonprofit plays a significant role in the community as the expert in a specific program area.
	3. The nonprofit can demonstrate cooperative efforts with business, government, education, health agencies, other nonprofits, faith based organizations, and unions.
✓	**VI. Core Element—Resource Development**
	1. The board has approved an anticoercion policy for fundraising.
	2. Fundraising strategies and results are examined after each fundraising project, with recommendations incorporated into the next effort.
	3. Fundraising strategies are used that will generate an 80 percent income and no more than 20 percent in expenses (including staff costs).

	4. No more than 20 percent of the budget comes from any single source or fundraising strategy.
	5. Board members are involved in fundraising.
	6. Board members are required to make a financial contribution to the nonprofit commiserate with their personal income level.
	7. Staff involved in fundraising regularly attends fundraising workshops to gather new ideas and expertise.
	8. Fundraising strategies are based on research that indicates the pros and cons of each strategy.
	9. A long-term planned giving program is in effect.
	10. A variety of fundraising strategies are used.
	11. To avoid burnout of volunteers and staff, no more than three fundraising events are conducted within one year.
✓	**VII. Core Element—Marketing**
	1. An annual, year-round marketing plan is being implemented.
	2. Marketing plans are based on a specific brand image the nonprofit wants to be conveyed.
	3. All publications and marketing materials consistently convey a message that enhances the mission.
	4. Marketing strategies are based on research.
	5. Marketing and publicity strategies use proven outcomes measurements of the programs to tell the "story" of the mission of the nonprofit.

Summary of Assessment

Enter the number of check marks you made for each category.

Number of Checks	Maximum Number	Category
		I. Basic Infrastructure
	9	Vision/mission/values
	3	Organizational structure
	10	Strategic planning
		II. Core Element—Administration
	4	Policies and procedures

Number of Checks	Maximum Number	Category
	20	Financial
	11	Human resources (personnel)
	4	Facilities and equipment
	11	Risk management
		III. Core Element—Board/Volunteer Development
	12	Board of directors
	5	Volunteer development
	9	**IV. Core Element—Programs**
	3	**V. Core Element—Community Involvement**
	11	**VI. Core Element—Resource Development**
	5	**VII. Core Element—Marketing**

Return this completed page to _____ **by the deadline in the cover letter or email.**

Name_____   **Board Member** ☐ **Staff** ☐

Note: For a simple analysis, look for categories with less than 50 percent of the statements checked in any category, which could indicate a weak area. Also look for differences between staff and board responses. The consultant or facilitator can use this summary to put together a bar chart that shows the comparison between staff and board answers, as shown.

Appendix D—Sample Financial Policies and Procedures

Date approved by the board of directors:_____

Advances

(See "Loans and Salary/Wages Advance.")

Accounting Policies and Procedures

(See **Chapter Three**.)

Allocation of Costs

All costs, to the extent possible, should be charged directly to the program(s) or internal function for which the costs are incurred. However, there are other costs (management and general) that are not identifiable with a single program or fundraising activity but are indispensable to the conduct of those activities and to the organization's existence. Such costs can include expenses for the overall direction of the organization's general board activities, business management, general record keeping, budget preparation, and related purposes. These internal operating costs will be allocated each year using the chart of accounts and the internal division percentages annually determined through the budget process and found in **Chapter Three**.

Management and general costs, as defined in SOP 78-10 (10,250.091), are "those not identifiable with a single program or fundraising activity but are indispensable to the conduct of those activities and to an organization's existence, including expenses for the overall direction of the organization's general board activities, business management, general record keeping, budgeting and related purposes. Costs of overall direction usually include the salary and expenses of the chief executive officer of the organization and his or her staff, unless time sheets show specific time periods directly involved in supervision of program services or categories of supporting services, then salaries and expenses should be prorated among those functions."

Audit

Every three years, at least three audit bids will be procured and reviewed by the administration committee, which will recommend to the board the auditor to conduct the annual audit for a three-year period. The auditor will present the audit to the administration committee for discussion and be available to respond to questions at a board meeting if requested. Funds for the audit will be included in the annual budget.

Authority

The executive director is authorized to act on behalf of the organization to sign contracts, leases, and other legal documents that singularly obligate the organization in an amount not to exceed $10,000. The board will be informed of such actions within thirty to ninety days of signature. The executive director will consult with the chair of the board and the executive committee within ninety days of such action. As part of the annual performance review of the executive director, the board will review the activity of the executive director to ensure the executive director has not exceeded the scope of the position's authority. In the absence of the executive director, the senior vice president is authorized to act on behalf of the organization and to sign checks. Contracts, leases, and other legal documents are not to be signed by the senior vice president without the written authorization of the executive director or the chair of the board.

Banking

- Funds are to be deposited with financial institutions that are donors to the nonprofit.

- Deposits are to be kept at a level that will allow for total FDIC or FSLIC insurance coverage (no account over $250,000).

- Changes in banking institutions and additions or closing of accounts must be approved by the board of directors.

- Board-authorized signature cards will be revised annually to reflect the changes in board officers or staff. Changes will also be made when any authorized signatories are no longer able to serve.

- The administration committee of the board of directors will annually review and recommend any changes in investment strategies.

- Bank statements will be reconciled within fifteen days of receipt and approved by the executive director or senior vice president.

- Canceled checks will be filed in numerical order and will include a copy of the disbursement journal.

- Deposits will not be made by the same person who opens the mail; a tally will be made of checks received by the person who opens the mail, and the tally will be presented with the checks to the internal operations staff person designated to make deposits.

Budget

- An annual budget will be approved by the board of directors and may include capital expenditures. The board must approve any expenditure above the total budget. The board will review the budget on a quarterly basis.

- The quarterly budget report to the administration committee will include month-by-month comparisons of actual with budget; quarterly reports to the board will include year-to-date actual compared budget.

- The annual budget will be developed by the executive director, with input from the division vice presidents.

- The budget will be developed by a review of the previous year's budget and projected actual compared with anticipated income and expenses for the coming fiscal year.

Conflict of Interest

◆ Board members or employee who have a financial interest in any business or organization doing business with the nonprofit shall declare to the board such potential conflict of interest and will remove themselves from any related decision-making by the board.

◆ Board members will be asked annually to sign the conflict-of-interest form, and a copy will be kept in their files.

◆ As part of the initial statement of understanding signed by employees upon their hiring by the nonprofit, they agree to adhere to the conflict-of-interest policy.

Disbursements/Expenses

◆ All disbursements, except those from petty cash, will be made by prenumbered checks. Unused checks will be kept in the locked, fireproof safe.

◆ Voided checks will be preserved and filed after appropriate mutilation of the signature area.

◆ No checks will be made payable to cash or bearer.

◆ No checks will be signed without all spaces completed (such as who it is made out to and the amount), and all checks require two board-approved signatures (preferably at least one volunteer's signature) for checks in any amounts over $5,000.

◆ All checks to be signed will include invoices clearly marked with the division supervisor's approval and the chart of accounts numbers (sample in procedures manual)

◆ All submitted invoices and supporting documents will be clearly marked paid, with the date and check number, and will be filed by the vendor, alphabetically (sample in procedures manual).

◆ All invoices are to be paid within thirty days to prevent penalties and ensure discounts. The executive director or senior vice president will be notified if any invoices will not be paid within thirty days, with written indication of the reason for the delay.

◆ Check requests will be made to the internal operations director at least two weeks in advance of the due date.

◆ Invoices will be checked to ensure sales tax is not being paid.

◆ Payroll tax deposits will be made within five working days of payroll disbursement.

◆ Any service or equipment purchases over $500 require at least three bids. A bid file will be kept on each vendor for future reference.

◆ All checks presented to signatories will include a memo showing the amount of cash available in all accounts before and after disbursements.

◆ The executive director and vice presidents of the organization are authorized to order goods or services on behalf of the organization. Any purchases over $500 will require prior written approval of the executive director to ensure the purchase is within budget limitations and to review the bids received.

◆ All checks are issued and mailed by the internal operations director, but all require the approval of the executive director or senior vice president before mailing.

Donated Services/Materials

◆ Donated services or materials will be recorded as revenue and expensed at the same amount.

◆ Donated services will not duplicate services performed by paid employees.

◆ Donated services will be supervised in the same manner and with the same controls and policies as paid staff, including the use of time sheets.

◆ Donated services and materials will be valued at the same rate as if they had been purchased, as determined by a written analysis and documentation from similar products or services.

Files

Following is the length of time to keep each type of file:

◆ IRS Form 990: ten years

◆ IRS Form 941: four years after due date

◆ Annual audit: permanent

◆ Insurance policies: five years after expiration or replacement of policy

◆ Accounts receivable: five years

◆ Accounts payable: three years

◆ Bank account records (statements, deposits, checks): five years

◆ Monthly financial reports: ten years

◆ Fixed-asset records: permanent

◆ Employee reimbursement records: three years

◆ State tax exemption: permanent

◆ IRS 501(c)(3): permanent

Financial Reports

◆ The treasurer will provide to the board of directors, at least quarterly, a financial statement in accordance with standards of accounting for nonprofits showing year-to-date budget and year-to-date actual and a balance sheet showing assets and liabilities. The report will be approved at a regularly called board meeting.

◆ If desired, internal monthly financial reports will be made available to staff and administration committee volunteers with quarterly financial reports prepared and made available by the outside accounting firm.

Insurance

◆ Directors and officers liability insurance, including volunteer and employee bonding, will be purchased annually by the organization.

◆ Insurance policies will be filed in a fireproof safe or safety deposit box.

◆ At least every other year, the administration committee will review all insurance policies to determine if they are adequate for the needs of the organization.

Internal Audit

At least quarterly, the senior vice president will do a random internal audit of the financial controls of the organization (see procedures manual "Internal Audit Checklist"). Findings from the audit will be discussed with the executive director and reported to the administration committee at the quarterly board of directors meeting. Board members or senior staff will also conduct random internal audits periodically.

Inventory/Assets Management

◆ A ledger of all capital equipment or property will be maintained, with appropriate depreciation amounts shown.

◆ An annual inventory of equipment will be conducted by the internal operations division and compared with the ledger. For publications whose total resale value is over $2,000, quarterly inventories will be taken.

◆ All new equipment/furniture will be marked with an inventory control number and the nonprofit identification.

◆ The base price for fixed assets is $500. Any items purchased for less should be charged to an expense account.

◆ Inventory counts will also include publications. A file will be maintained on every publication over 500 copies that will be sold. The file will include copies of bids, invoices paid, budget projections, copies of sales advertisements, etc.

◆ The executive director or senior vice president must approve all fixed-asset purchases.

Legal Forms/Reports

◆ A copy of the IRS tax-exempt, tax-deductible 501(c)(3) letter shall be filed in a safe or safety deposit box, along with copies of any required state documents (state tax exemption, incorporation papers, charitable registration, etc.).

◆ The board will annually review the organization's activities to ensure they are not engaged in any activities that are beyond the scope of the organization's charter or mission.

◆ The IRS 990 form will be filed with IRS and will be completed as part of the annual audit. Any unrelated business income will be reported on Form 990T.

◆ The IRS 5500 pension fund report form will be filed with IRS by July 31 of each year. The internal operations director or the executive director will prepare the pension fund report.

◆ The W-2 payroll forms will be filed with IRS in January, with copies to employees.

◆ Payroll taxes will be paid as a part of each payroll period's checks. Quarterly payroll reports will be filed with IRS.

Loans

Use of organizational funds for loans to volunteers or employees is strictly prohibited.

Payroll

◆ Wages and salaries will be paid twice a month (first and fifteenth). If these dates fall on a weekend or holiday, paychecks will be issued the last business day before the weekend or holiday.

◆ All wages and salaries will be based on a board-approved salary range for each position. A written statement of understanding, showing the agreed-upon salary/wage and any increases, will be placed in each employee's personnel file, with a copy to the internal operations director.

◆ Sick leave and vacation time accrued and used will be given in a written report to all employees at least monthly.

◆ Any deductions from a paycheck, other than the standard legal deductions for taxes, must be supported by a signed authorization from the employee. Such deductions might include charitable donations, telephone and copier use for personal matters, etc.

◆ Employees will annually complete a W-4 statement to ensure the proper numbers of deductions are used for payroll taxes. A copy of the W-4 will be placed in each employee's personnel file and in the internal operations payroll file.

◆ Policies regarding vacation, sick leave, or other time off are contained in the employee handbook.

◆ Payroll checks will be prepared and disbursed by the internal operations division but approved and signed by the executive director or senior vice president.

(See "Timesheets" for policies and procedures related to documentation of staff time.)

Personnel Policies

(See "Employee Handbook," **Appendix F**.)

Petty Cash

◆ The petty cash fund will not exceed $200 and is to be used for expenses not normally incurred through a regular vendor. Any expenditure from the petty cash fund will be justified by an expenditure receipt signed by the staff or volunteer requesting the funds.

◆ The executive director, a designated board member, or the senior vice president will approve petty cash reimbursement requests. Petty cash reimbursement will be by checks drawn on the regular bank account and made out to the custodian of the account. Access to petty cash will be limited to no more than two people, and someone other than the fund custodian will make a random count of petty cash at least quarterly.

◆ Except in unusual circumstances and authorization by the executive director, each petty cash disbursement will not exceed fifty dollars. No employee checks will be cashed out of the petty cash fund.

Pledges/Dues and Revenue

◆ Only amounts received will be recorded as revenue. Pledges will be recorded as accounts receivable, with an offsetting amount in deferred revenues.

◆ A thank-you letter will be issued in the donor's name within thirty days of receipt of the pledge or donation.

◆ Quarterly pledge verification statements will be issued on all outstanding pledges.

◆ An uncollectible report will be issued by the executive director annually to the board. The board will decide which uncollectibles are to be written off.

◆ Receivables written off as uncollectibles are carried in a separate ledger, and the executive director reviews collection efforts on a quarterly basis.

◆ Amounts due from employees or volunteers are invoiced at least quarterly, and uncollected invoices are reviewed quarterly by the executive committee and administration committee.

◆ Attempts will be made to segregate duties with regard to dues notices, access to cash receipts, or the authority to write off uncollectible accounts, although the small size of the current staff may warrant having the person sending dues notices be the same person with access to cash receipts. To prevent problems, the executive director or senior vice president will approve all dues notices.

Publications

A file will be maintained on every publication over 500 copies that will be sold. Annual inventories for audits will include counts of remaining publications. Quarterly inventories will be done on publications whose potential resale value is more than $2,000.

Receipts for Cash/Checks

◆ All persons having access to cash/checks will be bonded through directors and officers liability insurance.

◆ Incoming mail will be opened and disbursed by someone other than the person making bank deposits.

◆ All checks received will be immediately stamped "for deposit only" on the backs with the bank stamp and deposited within five working days. A listing of all cash and checks received will be made on a daily basis, with receipts issued to donors within five working days.

◆ The listing of cash/checks received will be forwarded to the accountant.

◆ All receipts for cash/checks will be issued from a prenumbered receipt book.

◆ Anticipated revenue sources are scheduled in advance so that nonreceipt by the due date can be promptly investigated.

◆ All negotiable assets are under the control of the executive director or designated board members.

◆ Deposit tickets validated by the bank will be compared with the cash/check receipts listing.

◆ Nonsufficient funds checks returned by the bank will be promptly investigated.

◆ Bank deposits are compared with the receipts book on a monthly basis.

◆ Until deposited, all receipts (cash and checks) will be kept in the locked, fireproof safe.

◆ Deposits will be made daily—unless the receipts are less than $200, then no less than weekly.

Reserves

As part of the annual budget development process, 5 percent of the gross revenue will be set aside until a six-month operating reserve is accumulated. The reserve funds will be put into a special account, with the use of the funds to be authorized by the board.

Restricted Funds

◆ Restricted gifts will be recorded in a separate fund, with adequate substantiation indicating the nature of the restriction and the time and circumstances under which such restrictions will lapse.

◆ The establishment of designated or restricted funds, and any expenditure of the funds, will be approved by the board of directors.

◆ There will be no borrowing from restricted funds.

Salary/Wage Advances

(See "Loans.")

Travel/Conference Expenses

◆ No expenses will be reimbursed without original receipts. The only exceptions are expenses where receipts are not available (like tips or split food tickets) but can be substantiated by other expenses, such as airline tickets, hotel, etc.

◆ Expense reports will be checked against receipts, and an adding machine tape showing substantiation will be stapled to the front of the expense report before paying.

◆ All expense reports/reimbursements will be approved by the employee's supervisor or a designated board member.

◆ Travel and other cash allowances paid to employees are reported as additional compensation on the employee's annual W-2 form.

◆ When corporate credit cards are used, they will be issued in the employee's name and will be used only for business expenses. Use of the corporate credit card for personal expenses is grounds for immediate dismissal. Employees who are provided with corporate credit cards will sign for them when issued and will also sign a statement regarding their not being used for personal use and the potential for immediate dismissal.

◆ Employees or volunteers will not be reimbursed for alcoholic beverages.

◆ Because corporate credit cards are available, travel advances will not be used.

Uncollectibles

◆ An annual report will be issued to the board showing outstanding receivables, including recommendations on which ones are to be categorized as uncollectibles.

◆ Any noncollectible donation pledges identified will be followed up with the donor, with a subsequent report to the board.

◆ Written pledge billings will be made quarterly. The executive director or senior vice president will make telephone calls for pledges that are more than six months overdue.

Appendix E—Sample Policies/Procedures Manual Checklist

Indicate with an "x" or a date when the policy/procedure has been finalized in the manual. This should not be regarded as a complete list but rather a sample of things to include.

Accounting

❑ Accounts payable procedures

❑ Billing procedures

❑ Bank deposit procedures

❑ Bid and contract policies/procedures

❑ Budget development procedures

❑ Travel expense reimbursement policies/procedures/forms

❑ Financial management policies/procedures

❑ Internal operations audit checklist

Board of Directors

❑ Sample meeting agendas

❑ Board/organization structure chart

❑ Officer job descriptions

❑ Nominating committee policies/procedures

❑ Board orientation procedures

❑ Board member satisfaction surveys

❑ Legal responsibilities of board members

❑ Sample conflict-of-interest statement

❑ Sample commitment-to-serve statement

❑ Board member job description

❑ Committee job descriptions

❑ Sample board member application

❑ Board demographics matrix

❑ Current list of board members and contact information

Employees

❑ Hiring packets (including I-9, W-4, benefits sign-up, employee handbook signature page, payroll deduction forms, etc.)

❑ Procedures for updating employee handbook

❑ Procedures/policies related to hiring/firing (job applications, exit interviews)

❑ Board-approved job descriptions for all positions

❑ Board-approved salary ranges for all positions

❑ Procedures for updating job descriptions and salary ranges

❑ Performance review policies and procedures

❑ Executive director performance review policies and procedures

❑ Parking policies and procedures

❑ Policies and procedures related to the building (entrance hours, safety, etc.)

Email

Policies and procedures related to the use of email, including personal use of company computers for email.

Equipment

❑ Vendor files (including contracts, maintenance agreements, etc.)

❑ Instruction manuals

Files

❑ Database procedures (changing, adding, etc.)

❑ Mail-merge procedures

❑ Client files (policies and procedures related to their use)

❑ Board member files

❑ Length of time to keep files

❑ Accounting files

❑ Other filing systems

Internet

❑ Policies and procedures related to the business and personal use of the Internet

Mailings

❑ Procedures for any regular mailings (small and large)

❑ When and how to using bulk rate for mailings

Meetings

❑ Annual meeting, sample agendas/minutes

❑ Annual report samples

❑ Board meeting procedures/agendas/minutes

❑ Committee meeting procedures/agendas/minutes

❑ Meeting checklist for room arrangements, food, audiovisuals, etc.

Office Supplies

❑ Policies/procedures for ordering of office supplies

❑ List of vendors usually used and why

Publications

❑ Samples of all publications produced by the organization

❑ Vendor files for printers

Strategic Plan

❑ Policies/procedures/timelines for strategic plan development and response to unexpected changes in the nonprofit's environment

Timeline

❑ Organizational timelines (weekly, monthly, annual, etc.)

❑ Executive director timelines

Volunteers (Committee, Program, and Board)

❑ Recruitment policies/procedures

❑ Training policies/procedures

❑ Recognition policies/procedures

❑ Dismissal policies/procedures

Appendix F—Sample Personnel Policies and Employee Handbook

This handbook is meant to be an example only. Be sure you have your final policies and the handbook checked by an attorney familiar with the law of tax-exempt organizations and labor laws, as state and federal employee laws in the United States change often. If you are outside the United States, it is also critical that you have the policies by an attorney or government official familiar with the labor laws of your country, state, or province. Once the final document is approved by the governing board, add a table of contents at the beginning to make the handbook easier to use.

Date approved by the board:_____

Welcome!

On behalf of your colleagues, I welcome you to (the nonprofit) and wish you every success in your new job. We believe that each employee contributes directly to the nonprofit's success, and we hope you will take pride in being a member of our team.

This handbook was developed to describe some of the expectations of our employees and to outline the policies, programs, and benefits available to eligible employees. Employees should familiarize themselves with the contents of the employee handbook as soon as possible, for it will answer many questions about employment with (nonprofit). Once you have reviewed the information, please sign, date, and return Attachment B.

We hope that your experience here will be challenging, enjoyable, and rewarding.

_____ (executive director's signature)

Introduction

An interesting and challenging experience awaits you as an employee of (nonprofit name), hereafter referred to as the nonprofit. We have written this handbook to answer some of the questions you may have concerning the policies of the nonprofit. Please read it thoroughly and retain it for future reference. Should you have any questions regarding any policies, please ask the on-site supervisor.

101 Notice to Employees

This employee handbook supersedes all previous nonprofit handbooks and policies. Also, this handbook supersedes all prior management memos to the extent that such memo contradicts a subject or policy covered therein.

102 Changes in Policies

The policies in this handbook are subject to change at the sole discretion of the nonprofit board. We will notify you of these changes by appropriate means. Changes will be effective on dates determined by the nonprofit, and you must not rely on policies that have been superseded. No supervisor or manager has any authority to alter the foregoing. If you are uncertain about any policy or procedure, please check with the on-site supervisor.

Employment

201 Nature of Employment

The on-site supervisor may delegate responsibilities contained in these policies to other supervisory personnel.

This handbook is not a contract guaranteeing employment for any specific duration. Both you and the nonprofit have the right to terminate your employment at any time. No supervisor, manager, or representative of the nonprofit, other than the executive director or designated board member, has the authority to enter into any agreement for employment for any specified period or to make any promises or commitments contrary to the foregoing. Any employment agreement entered into by the executive director or board member shall not be enforceable unless it is in writing and signed by both parties.

All provisions in this handbook are subject to revisions of applicable local, state, and federal laws. Any provision that may become unlawful under subsequent law shall be void and unenforceable. It is inevitable that new policies will need to be written from time to time and that old policies will need to be revised. While the nonprofit reserves the right to make changes in this handbook or in nonprofit policy without notice, we will strive to provide you with those revisions promptly. The only recognized deviations from the stated policies are those authorized and signed by the executive director of this nonprofit and approved by the board.

202 Employee Relations

The employer believes that the work conditions, wages, and benefits it offers to its employees are competitive with those offered by other employers in this area and in this industry. If employees have any concerns about work conditions or compensation, they are strongly encouraged to voice these concerns openly and directly to their supervisors.

Experience has shown that when employees deal directly with supervisors, the work environment is excellent, communications are clear, and attitudes are positive. The nonprofit believes it has amply demonstrated its commitment to responding effectively to all employee concerns.

203 Equal Employment Opportunity

The nonprofit has been, and continues to be, morally and legally committed to the principle of equal employment opportunity. It is the policy of this nonprofit to ensure that all employment decisions shall be based on merit, qualifications, and competence. Except where required or permitted by law, employment practices shall not be influenced or affected by virtue of an applicant's or employee's race, color, creed, age, sex, national origin or ancestry, marital status, veteran status, status as a qualified disabled or handicapped individual, or any other characteristic protected by law.

It is the employer's policy to provide an environment that is free of unlawful harassment of any kind, including that which is sexual or related to age or ethnicity. This policy governs all aspects of employment, promotion, assignment, discharge, and other terms and conditions of employment.

The nonprofit provides equal employment opportunities to all employees and applicants without regard to race, color, sex, national origin, age, disability, military status, or status as a Vietnam-era or special disabled veteran in accordance with applicable federal and state laws.

The nonprofit complies with applicable state and local laws governing nondiscrimination in employment in every location in which the nonprofit has facilities. This policy applies to all terms and conditions of employment, including, but not limited to, hiring, placement, promotion, termination, layoff, recall, transfers, leave of absence, compensation, and training.

204 Personnel Files

The nonprofit maintains a personnel file on each employee. You may review your personnel file upon request and in the presence of authorized personnel. If you are interested in reviewing your file, contact your payroll specialist to make arrangements.

To ensure that your personnel file is up to date at all times, notify your supervisor or your payroll specialist of any changes in your name, telephone number, home address, marital status, number of dependents, beneficiary designations, scholastic achievements, the individuals to notify in case of an emergency, and so forth. An Employee Change in Status Notice will need to be filled out and sent to the Internal Operations Department.

Personnel files are the property of the employer, and access to the information they contain is restricted. Generally, only officials and representatives of the employer have a legitimate reason to review information in a file.

205 Employment of Relatives

The nonprofit permits the employment of qualified relatives of employees as long as such employment does not, in the opinion of the nonprofit, create actual or perceived conflicts of interest. Favoritism to relatives is unfair to other employees, and the appearance of favoritism is easily perceived. Although the nonprofit has no prohibition against hiring relatives of existing employees, we are committed to monitoring situations in which relatives work in the same area. In case of actual or potential problems, the employer will take prompt action.

For purposes of this policy, "relative" is defined as a spouse, child, parent, sibling, grandparent, grandchild, aunt, uncle, first cousin, or corresponding in-law or "step" relation. The nonprofit will exercise sound business judgment in the placement of related employees in accordance with the following guidelines:

◆ Individuals who are related by blood or marriage are permitted to work in the same nonprofit facility, provided no direct reporting or supervisory or management relationship exists. That is, no employee is permitted to work within the "chain of command" of a relative such that the other relative could influence one relative's work responsibilities, salary, or career progress.

◆ No relatives are permitted to work in the same department or in any other positions in which the nonprofit believes an inherent conflict of interest may exist.

◆ Employees who marry while employed are treated in accordance with these guidelines. That is, if, in the opinion of the nonprofit, a conflict or an apparent conflict arises as a result of the marriage, one of the employees will be transferred at the earliest practicable time. If transfer is not possible, termination of one or both of the employees may be necessary.

◆ Employees with decision-making authority will avoid selecting consultants or service providers who are relatives or personal friends or who employ or are affiliated with relatives or personal friends.

This policy applies to all categories of employment at the nonprofit, including regular, temporary, and part-time classifications.

206 Immigration Law Compliance

This nonprofit is committed to employing only US citizens and aliens who are authorized to work in the United States and who comply with the Immigration Reform and Control Act of 1986.

As a condition of employment, each new employee must properly complete, sign, and date the first section of the Immigration and Naturalization Service Form I-9 within three business days after employment. Before commencing work, newly rehired employees must also complete the form if they have not previously filed an I-9 with this nonprofit, if their previous I-9 is more than three years old, or if their previous I-9 is no longer valid. This procedure has been established by law and requires that every individual provide satisfactory evidence of his or her identity and legal authorization to work in the United States.

207 Conflicts of Interest

To avoid even the appearance of a conflict of interest that would tarnish the image of the nonprofit and undermine the public's trust in all organizations, nonprofit employees will avoid any activity or outside interest that conflicts or appears to conflict with the best interests of the nonprofit.

Any involvement with a current or potential vendor, grantee, or competing program may violate this code and should be cleared with the employee's supervisor; employees will refrain from participation in or being influenced by any decision or other action of the nonprofit that could result in a direct or indirect benefit to the employee's family or any program with which the employee is substantially affiliated.

208 Outside Employment

An employee may hold a second job with another program as long as the employee's job responsibilities with this nonprofit are performed satisfactorily. Employees should consider the impact outside employment could have on their health and physical endurance. All employees will be judged by the same performance standards and will be subject to the employer's scheduling demands regardless of any existing outside work requirements.

If the employer determines that an employee's outside work interferes with performance or the ability to meet the requirements of this nonprofit as they are modified from time to time, the employee may be asked to terminate the outside employment to remain with this nonprofit.

Written notification of secondary employment must be given to the supervisor. This notification is solely for determining possible conflicts of interest. Outside employment will present a conflict of interest if it has an actual or potential adverse impact on this nonprofit.

209 Nondisclosures

The protection of confidential information and discussions is vital to the interest and the success of this nonprofit. Any employee who discloses confidential information will be subject to disciplinary action (including possible discharge), even if the employee does not actually benefit from the disclosed information.

210 Amendments to This Handbook

The policies contained in this handbook may be changed as management deems necessary. While it is desirable to provide advance notice of such changes, it may not always be possible to do so. Do not consider this handbook to be a fixed document. The nonprofit reserves the right to make changes as needed. Refer any questions concerning policy changes or interpretation to the executive director. Changes and interpretations can be made only by action of the board and can be issued only in a written memo or letter signed by the executive director (or the chair of the board). Employees will be notified in writing of any changes to the handbook.

Employment Status and Records

301 Employee Categories

It is the intent of the employer to clarify the definitions of employment classifications so the employees understand their employment status and benefit eligibility. These classifications do not guarantee employment for any specified period of time. Accordingly, the right to terminate the employment relationship at will at any time is retained by both the employee and the employer.

The law requires *exempt* employees to work in an administrative, executive, or professional capacity. An administrative employee is one whose primary duty is performing office or nonmanual work that is directly related to the management or general operation of the nonprofit, who regularly exercises independent judgment and discretion, and regularly assists a bona fide executive or administrative employee, or one who does special or technical work requiring special experience, training, or knowledge, or who performs special assignments under general supervision only.

An executive employee primarily engages in managerial responsibilities, regularly and customarily supervises two or more workers, either has hiring and firing authority or makes recommendations about hiring and firing that are given special consideration, and regularly and customarily exercises discretionary powers.

Professional employees have a primary duty of performing work requiring advanced knowledge acquired after a long course of special instruction rather than through a general academic education and requires the exercise of judgment or discretion. If you have any question about your particular classification, please ask your supervisor.

Nonexempt employees are entitled to overtime pay under the specific provisions of federal and state laws. *Exempt* employees are excluded from specific provisions of federal and state wage and hour laws. *Exempt* employees shall be considered to be employed in an administrative, executive, or professional capacity. (Note: There are some legal battles in the US courts about this issue, so be sure to check with an attorney familiar with labor laws before finalizing this section of the handbook.) In addition to the above categories, each employee will belong to one other employee category:

◆ *Regular full-time* employees are those who are not in a temporary or introductory period status and who work the nonprofit's regularly scheduled workweek. Generally, they are eligible for the employer's benefits package and are subject to the terms, conditions, and limitations of each benefit program.

◆ *Regular part-time* employees are those who are not assigned to a temporary or introductory period status and who are regularly scheduled to work less than the full-time work schedule but at least twenty hours per week. Regular part-time employees are eligible for some benefits sponsored by the employer, subject to the terms, conditions, and limitations of each benefit program.

◆ *Part-time* employees are those who are not assigned to a temporary or introductory period status and who are scheduled to work fewer than twenty hours per week. While they do receive all legally mandated benefits (such as workers' compensation and Social Security benefits), they are ineligible for all the employer's other benefit programs.

All new and rehired employees will have an initial trial service period of ninety days. An employee will use this initial period after being hired, rehired, or accepting another position at the nonprofit to determine whether the new position meets the employee's expectations. The employer uses this period to evaluate employee capabilities, attitude, and work habits. Either the employee or the employer may end the employment relationship at will at any time during or after the introductory period, with or without cause or advance notice.

Employment with this nonprofit is at the mutual consent of the employer and the employee, and either party may terminate that relationship at any time, with or without cause and with or without advance notice.

302 Overtime for Nonexempt Employees

It should be recognized by all employees that overtime and additional work other than that which is regularly scheduled may be required. Overtime will be paid to eligible, nonexempt employees in accordance with applicable state law. The pay for regular overtime will be at the federal or state prescribed wage rate, whichever is higher.

All overtime must be authorized before its occurrence by your immediate supervisor. All overtime will be clearly noted on your time sheet and should be initialed on a daily basis by your immediate supervisor.

303 Employment Reference and Criminal Background Checks

To ensure that individuals who join the nonprofit are well qualified and have a strong potential to be productive and successful, it is the policy of the employer to check the employment references and criminal backgrounds of all applicants.

The nonprofit will respond to reference check inquiries on current and previous employees if:

◆ the request is in writing; or

◆ the request is by telephone and the correct Social Security number is provided.

Responses to such inquiries will confirm only dates of employment, wage rates or salary ranges, position(s) held, and whether or not you would rehire them.

304 Employee Applications

The employer relies upon the accuracy of information contained in the employment application as well as the accuracy of other data presented throughout the hiring process and employment. Any misrepresentations, falsifications, or material omissions in any of this information or data will result in the employer's exclusion of the individual from further consideration for employment or, if the person has been hired, termination of employment.

305 Performance Evaluations

You will be evaluated with respect to the job that you are performing for the nonprofit. As you demonstrate the ability to take on additional responsibilities, your talents will be utilized in the manner deemed most suitable to your demonstrated ability and the needs of the nonprofit.

Supervisors and employees are strongly encouraged to discuss job performance and goals on an informal, day-to-day basis. Additional formal performance reviews are conducted to provide both supervisors and employees the opportunity to discuss job tasks, identify and correct weaknesses, encourage and recognize strengths, and discuss positive, purposeful approaches for meeting goals. The performance of all employees is evaluated according to an ongoing twelve-month cycle, generally beginning at the fiscal year-end.

Merit-based pay adjustments are awarded by this nonprofit to recognize truly superior employee performance. The decision to award such an adjustment is dependent upon numerous factors, including the information documented by the Employee Performance Plan (Attachment A).

Employee Benefit Programs

401 Employee Benefits

Eligible employees in this nonprofit are provided a wide range of benefits. A number of the programs (such as Social Security, workers' compensation, state disability, and unemployment insurance) cover all employees in the manner prescribed by law.

Benefits eligibility is dependent upon a variety of factors, including employee classification. The actual terms and conditions of each benefit are governed by the actual statute or policy granting the benefit. Nothing herein should be interpreted as changing those terms. The nonprofit reserves the right at any time without notice to cancel in its entirety employee benefits or to modify the amount or scope thereof. Your supervisor can identify the benefits for which you are eligible. Details of many of these benefits can be found elsewhere in the employee handbook.

402 Vacation Benefits

All full-time regular employees will begin accruing vacation from the date of hire. Accumulation rates will be computed as follows:

Completed Years of Service	Annual Rate
One through five	Ten working days
Six through nine	Fifteen working days
Ten or more	Twenty working days

Employees are not eligible to take a vacation until after completing six months of employment. Vacation time cannot be used in advance.

Vacation pay will be calculated based on the employee's straight-time pay rate (in effect when vacation benefits are used) times the number of hours the employee would otherwise have worked on the day(s) of absence. Vacation pay does not include incentive pay, bonuses, or other special forms of compensation. Vacation benefits for salaried employees will be based on their normal wages.

If a scheduled holiday falls on a workday during the vacation period, this will entitle the employee to a corresponding number of additional days of vacation.

Vacations will be scheduled in advance with the employee's supervisor. Requests for vacation will be evaluated based on a number of factors, including anticipated operational requirements and staffing considerations during the requested vacation.

Employees are expected to use earned vacation within the year it applies. Vacation accumulation carryover from year to year will be limited to fifteen days and must be approved by the supervisor in advance.

Upon separation from employment, employees will be reimbursed for all accumulated vacation time at the wage or salary rate at the time of separation. Reconciliation and release of accumulated vacation pay will transpire on the first payday after separation.

The nonprofit recognizes prior service with other agencies and nonprofits when determining vacation and retirement benefits.

403 Holidays

The employer will grant holiday time off with pay to all eligible employees on the holidays listed below:

- ◆ New Year's Day: January 1
- ◆ Martin Luther King Jr. Day: third Monday in January
- ◆ Memorial Day: last Monday in May
- ◆ Independence Day: July 4
- ◆ Labor Day: first Monday in September
- ◆ Thanksgiving Day: fourth Thursday in November
- ◆ Day after Thanksgiving: fourth Friday in November
- ◆ Christmas Eve Day: December 24
- ◆ Christmas Day: December 25
- ◆ New Year's Eve: December 31

Should a holiday fall on a Saturday, the nonprofit will generally observe the occasion on the preceding Friday. Should a holiday occur on Sunday, the nonprofit will generally observe the occasion on the following Monday.

All eligible employees will receive one personal day off. An eligible nonexempt employee who works on a recognized holiday will receive holiday pay that is twice the employee's straight-time rate for the hours worked on the holiday. Prior approval must be obtained from the employee's supervisor.

404 Workers' Compensation Insurance

To provide for the payment of your medical expenses and for partial salary continuation in the event of work-related accident or illness, you are covered by workers' compensation insurance.

The amount of benefits payable and the duration of payment depend upon the nature of your injury or illness. However, all medical expenses incurred in connection with an on-the-job injury or illness and partial salary payments are paid in accordance with applicable state law.

If you are injured or become ill on the job, you must immediately report such injury or illness to the on-site supervisor. This ensures the nonprofit can help you obtain appropriate medical treatment. Failure to follow this procedure may result in the appropriate workers' compensation report not being filed in accordance with the law, which may delay benefits in connection with your injury or illness.

Questions regarding workers' compensation insurance should be directed to the on-site supervisor. The employer provides a workers' compensation insurance program at no cost to the employee. This program covers any injury or illness sustained in the course of employment that requires medical, surgical, or hospital treatment. Subject to applicable legal requirements, workers' compensation insurance provides benefits after a short waiting period or, if the employee is hospitalized, immediately.

405 Sick Leave Benefits

(Note: Many employers are converting to "Personal Time Off," in which they lump sick leave, vacation time, and personal days.)

The employer provides paid sick leave benefits to all eligible regular full-time employees for periods of temporary absence due to illnesses or injuries. Eligible employees will accrue sick leave benefits at the rate of ten hours per month. An eligible employee may use sick leave benefits for an absence due to illness or injury sustained by either that employee or a family member who resides in the employee's household. Sick leave is also used for doctors' appointments by an employee or a family member who resides in the employee's household.

Employees who are unable to report to work due to an illness or injury should notify their supervisor before the scheduled start time, if possible. The supervisor should also be contacted each additional day of absence. If an employee is absent for three or more consecutive days due to illness or injury, the supervisor may request a physician's statement verifying the nature of the disability and its beginning and expected ending dates. Such verification may be requested for other sick leave absences as well and will be the basis for payment authorization of sick leave benefits. Before returning to work from a sick leave absence of five calendar days or more, an employee may be asked to provide a physician's verification that the employee may safely return to work.

If an employee is eligible for basic unemployment/compensation disability (UCD) benefits, employer-paid sick leave shall be reduced by the amount of the UCD payment the employee is eligible to receive. This same method of integrated benefits shall also apply to an employee eligible for workers' compensation insurance payments.

Employees who receive full sick leave and are subsequently reimbursed by UCD or workers' compensation insurance benefits will have their pay adjusted by the amount of overpayment and their sick leave adjusted proportionately.

Unused sick leave benefits will be allowed to accumulate until the employee has accrued a total of 120 working days (six months) of sick leave benefits. Further accrual of sick leave benefits will be suspended until the employee has reduced the balance below this limit. Because sick leave benefits are intended to provide income protection in the event of an actual illness or injury, unused sick leave benefits cannot be used for any other paid or unpaid absence and will not be paid at the time of termination of employment or retirement.

406 Bereavement Leave

Regular full-time employees will receive leave with pay when a death occurs in the immediate family. Up to four days of leave will be granted at the death of members of the employee's immediate family, including spouse, children, parents, siblings, or persons related by marriage, including in-laws.

Bereavement pay is calculated based on the base pay that an employee would otherwise have earned had he or she worked on the day of absence. Approval of bereavement leave will occur in the absence of unusual operating requirements. Any employee may, with the supervisor's approval, use any available paid leave for additional time off as necessary.

407 Jury Duty

All full-time employees who serve on jury duty will be compensated by the nonprofit for the difference between the pay for jury duty (excluding mileage and travel fees) and their regular rate of pay. Employees must present the jury duty summons to their supervisor as soon as possible so that the supervisor may make arrangements to accommodate their absence. Either the employer or an employee may request an excuse from jury duty if, in the employer's judgment, the employee's absence would create difficulties. The employee is expected to report for work whenever the court schedule permits and should provide the supervisor with verification of any pay received from the court.

408 Witness Leave

The employer encourages employees to appear in court for witness duty whenever subpoenaed to do so. Employees will be granted unpaid time off for absence due to witness duty. Employees are free to use any available paid leave benefit (e.g., vacation leave) to receive compensation for the period of this absence.

The subpoena will be shown to the employee's supervisor after it is received so that operating requirements can be adjusted, when necessary, to accommodate the employee's absence. The employee is expected to report for work whenever the court schedule permits. If subpoenaed as a witness of the employer as a result of a job-related event, an employee will receive paid time off for the entire period of witness duty.

409 Retirement Benefits

The employer provides a retirement plan subject to length of service and employment by prior religious programs or nonprofits. (See retirement plan for specifics.)

Timekeeping/Payroll

501 Timekeeping

Accurately recording time worked is the responsibility of every employee. Federal and state laws require the employer to keep an accurate record of time worked in order to calculate employee pay and benefits. Time worked is all the time actually spent on the job performing assigned duties.

All employees will maintain accurate records of time worked. These time sheets will be the basis for the release of payroll money for nonexempt staff and for all staff for program cost accounting. It is the employee's responsibility to sign his or her time record to certify the accuracy of all time recorded. The supervisor will review and then initial the time record; both the employee and the supervisor must verify the accuracy of the changes by initialing the time record. Tampering, altering, or falsifying time records will result in disciplinary action, including potential discharge.

502 Payday

All employees are paid semimonthly on the fifteenth and the end of the month or on the preceding working day when payday falls on a Saturday, Sunday, or holiday.

503 Employee Terminations

Your employment with the nonprofit is voluntarily entered into, and you are free to resign at any time. Similarly, the nonprofit is free to conclude an employment relationship at any time at the sole discretion of the executive director. No one other than the executive director has the authority to make an agreement that conflicts with the above, and any such agreement must be in writing.

504 Administrative Pay Corrections

The employer takes all reasonable steps to ensure that employees receive the correct amount of pay in each paycheck and that employees are paid promptly on the scheduled payday.

In the unlikely event that there is an error in the amount of pay, the employee should promptly bring the discrepancy to the attention of the employer so that corrections can be made as quickly as possible.

505 Pay Deductions

The law requires that the employer make certain deductions from every employee's compensation. Among these are applicable federal, state, and local income taxes.

The employer offers benefits beyond those required by law. Eligible employees may voluntarily authorize deductions from their paychecks to cover the costs of participating in these programs. Under state law, all nontax and non-court-ordered deductions from employees' paychecks must be authorized in writing and signed by the employees. If you have questions concerning why deductions were made from your paycheck or how they were calculated, your supervisor can assist in having your questions answered.

Work Conditions and Hours

601 Safety

It is the policy of the nonprofit that accident prevention shall be considered of primary importance in all phases of operation and internal operations.

Establishment and maintenance of a safe work environment are the shared responsibility of the employer and employees at all levels of the nonprofit. The employer will attempt to do everything within its control to ensure a safe environment and compliance with federal, state, and local safety regulations. Employees are expected to obey safety rules and to exercise caution in all their work activities. They are asked to immediately report any unsafe conditions to their supervisor. Not only supervisors but also employees at all levels of the nonprofit are expected to correct unsafe conditions as promptly as possible.

All accidents that result in injury must be reported immediately to your supervisor, regardless of how insignificant the injury may appear. Such reports are necessary to comply with laws and initiate insurance and workers' compensation procedures. Any injury that occurs on the job, even a slight cut or strain, must be reported to management as soon as possible. In no circumstance, except an emergency, should an employee leave a workday without reporting an injury that occurred.

It is the intent of management to provide safe and healthy working conditions and to establish and insist upon safe practices at all times by all employees. The prevention of accidents is an objective affecting all levels of the nonprofit and its activities. It is, therefore, a basic requirement that each supervisor make the safety of employees an integral part of the supervisor's regular management function. The employer will attempt to do everything within its control to ensure a safe environment and compliance with federal, state, and local safety regulations.

Every effort will be made to provide adequate training to employees. However, if an employee is ever in doubt about how to do a job safely, it is the employee's duty to the supervisor for assistance. Safety is everyone's responsibility. Every supervisor is expected to devote the time and effort necessary to ensure the safety of employees at all times.

Responsibilities of the employee include the following:

◆ Obeying the safety rules

◆ Following safe job procedures (not taking shortcuts)

◆ Keeping work areas clean and free from slipping or tripping hazards

◆ Using prescribed personal protective equipment

◆ Immediately reporting all malfunctions to a supervisor

◆ Using care when lifting and carrying objects

◆ Observing restricted areas and all warning signs

◆ Knowing emergency procedures

◆ Reporting unsafe conditions to supervisors

◆ Promptly reporting every accident and injury to the supervisor

◆ Following the care prescribed by the attending physician when treated for an injury or illness

◆ Attending all employee safety meetings

◆ Participating in accident investigations

◆ Serving on safety committee or other loss control activities as needed

Failure to observe these guidelines may result in disciplinary action, up to and including termination of your employment.

602 Accidents

No matter how insignificant an injury may seem at the time of occurrence, you should notify the on-site supervisor immediately.

603 Safe Workplace Policy

It is the intent of the nonprofit to provide a safe workplace for employees and to provide a comfortable and secure atmosphere for members and others with whom we do programs. The nonprofit has a no-tolerance guideline for violent acts or threats of violence. The nonprofit expects all employees to conduct themselves in a threatening, nonthreatening, nonabusive manner at all times. No direct, conditional, or veiled threat of harm to any employee or nonprofit property will be considered acceptable behavior.

Acts of violence or intimidation of others will not be tolerated. Any employee who commits or threatens to commit a violent act against any person while on nonprofit premises will be subject to immediate discharge. If an employee while engaged in nonprofit business off the premises commits or threatens to commit a violent act, that employee will be subject to immediate discharge if the threat or violent act could adversely affect the nonprofit or its reputation in the community.

Employees share the responsibility in the identification and alleviation of threatening or violent behaviors. Any employee who is subjected to or threatened with violence, or who is aware of another individual who has been subjected to or threatened with violence, shall immediately report this information to their supervisor or a member of management.

Employees should not assume that any threat is not serious. If you as an individual feel threatened and need protection, do not hesitate to report the situation to a supervisor. Any threat reported to a supervisor should be brought to the attention of the HR department. HR will carefully investigate all reports, and employee confidentiality will be maintained to the fullest extent possible.

604 Work Schedule

The normal work schedule for all regular full-time employees is forty hours per week. Supervisors will advise all employees of the times their schedules will normally begin and end. Staffing needs and operational demands may necessitate variations in starting and ending times, as well as variations in the total hours that may be scheduled each day and week.

605 Communications Systems

It is the intent of the nonprofit to provide the communication systems necessary for the conduct of its business. Employees are expected to adhere to the proper use of all communication systems, including, but not limited to, the telephone, electronic mail (email), and voice mail.

The communication systems are owned and operated by the nonprofit and are to be used for the business of the nonprofit. Employees should have no expectation of privacy of any correspondence, messages, or information in the systems.

All telephone, email, and voice mail messages are the property of the nonprofit. The nonprofit reserves the right to access and disclose all such messages sent for any purpose. All such messages, regardless of content or the intent of the sender, are a form of corporate correspondence and are subject to the same internal and external regulation, security, and scrutiny as any other corporate correspondence. Except as identified, the nonprofit's communication systems will not be used to solicit or to address employees regarding commercial, religious, or political causes; nor will the system be used in ways that are disruptive or offensive to others.

Employees will not attempt to gain access to another employee's personal telephone, email, or voice mail messages. However, the nonprofit reserves the right to access an employee's messages at any time, without notice to the employee. Transmission of sexually explicit images, messages, cartoons, ethnic slurs, racial epithets, or anything that may be construed as harassment or disparagement of others based on race, national origin, sex, sexual orientation, age, disability, or religious or political beliefs, is specifically prohibited. Any violation of these guidelines may result in disciplinary action, up to and including termination. Searches of the Internet are not allowed unless the search is directly related to the employee's job responsibilities.

606 Personal and Business Phone Calls, Use of Equipment

During business hours, employees are requested to keep personal calls to an absolute minimum. If an employee needs to leave the workstation to conduct personal business, the employee must first obtain permission from an immediate supervisor. This will keep the supervisor aware of your activities during the day and allow modifications to be made to the work schedule if necessary.

Telephones are intended primarily for business and should not be tied up with personal calls. If the telephone is used for important personal matters, the number and length of calls should be limited. Personal texting is not allowed during working hours.

Employees will be required to reimburse the employer for any charges resulting from their personal use of the telephone, facsimile, mailing system, and photocopying machines. Employees will also be required to reimburse the employer for any other equipment or materials used. Personal mail and merchandise deliveries should be kept to a minimum. The nonprofit's address may be used as an employee's personal address only in unusual and temporary situations.

607 Rest and Meal Periods

Each workday, nonexempt employees are entitled to a fifteen-minute rest period for every four hours worked. Supervisors will advise employees of the regular rest period length and schedule. To the extent possible, rest periods will be provided in the middle of work periods.

All regular full-time nonexempt employees are provided with one meal period of sixty minutes in length each workday. Supervisors will schedule meal periods to accommodate operating requirements. Employees will be relieved of all active responsibilities and restrictions during meal periods and will not be compensated for that time.

608 Overtime

When operating requirements or other needs cannot be met during regular working hours, nonexempt employees will be given the opportunity to volunteer for overtime work assignments. All overtime work must receive the supervisor's prior authorization. Overtime assignments will be distributed as equitably as practical to all nonexempt employees qualified to perform the required work, and overtime will be paid at time-and-a-half straight-time rate for hours worked.

As required by law, overtime pay is based on actual hours worked over forty hours in a workweek. Time off for sick leave, vacation leave, or any leave of absence will not be considered hours worked for purposes of performing overtime pay calculations.

Compensatory time off (CTO) will be allowed under the following conditions:

◆ Before working overtime, the employee must voluntarily request in writing that CTO be granted instead of overtime compensation.

◆ In making such a request, the employee must clearly state in writing the wish to be compensated at the overtime rate in the form of time off from work rather than in the form of monetary compensation.

◆ CTO must be used in the same seven-day period that the overtime was worked. The time off must be given during normal working hours. Records must be kept that accurately reflect overtime earned and taken.

609 Use of Equipment

Equipment essential to accomplish job duties is often expensive and may be difficult to replace. When using property, employees are expected to exercise care, perform required maintenance, and follow all operating instructions, safety standards, and guidelines.

Notify the designated employee if any equipment, machines, or tools appear to be damaged, defective, or in need of repair. Prompt reporting of damages, defects, and the need for repairs could prevent deterioration of equipment and possible injury to employees or others.

The improper, careless, negligent, destructive, or unsafe use or operation of equipment will result in disciplinary action, including possible discharge.

Leaves of Absence

701 Family and Medical Leave

The nonprofit grants family and medical leaves of absence to eligible employees for the following:

◆ The birth of an employee's child or to care for the newborn child

◆ The placement of a child with the employee for adoption or state-approved foster care

◆ The care of an employee's spouse, child, or parent (family member) who has a serious health condition

◆ The employee's serious health condition that prevents the employee from performing any one essential function of the employee's position. A serious health condition is an illness, injury, impairment, or physical or mental condition that involves either inpatient care or continuing treatment by a health care provider.

Eligible Employee

An active full-time or part-time employee is eligible for family and medical leave under the Family and Medical Leave Act of 1993 provided that on the date leave is requested, the employee has been employed by the nonprofit at least twelve months and has worked at least 1,250 hours during the twelve-month period immediately preceding the commencement of leave.

Length of Leave

An eligible employee is entitled to a total of twelve workweeks of unpaid leave within a twelve-month period. The amount of leave available to an employee will be calculated by looking backward at the amount of leave taken within the twelve-month period immediately preceding the first date of leave.

Leave taken for the care of a newborn child or placement for adoption or foster care must be taken as an uninterrupted continuous leave of absence and must be taken within twelve months of the birth or placement of the child.

If both a husband and wife are employed by the nonprofit and are eligible for leave, except for leave due to the employee's serious health condition, the two may take a combined total of twelve weeks.

Intermittent leave or a reduced schedule may be approved for the employee's serious health condition or a family member's serious health condition when medically necessary and the need for such leave is best accommodated through such scheduling.

An employee requesting intermittent leave/reduced schedule may be transferred temporarily to an available alternative position with equivalent pay and benefits or to a part-time position if such a position better accommodates the need for intermittent leave/reduced schedule.

Employee Notification Requirements

If an employee expects to take family and medical leave, the employee must notify the nonprofit of the intention to take leave at least thirty days in advance of the expected leave. Following proper notification, the employee must complete a Leave of Absence Request form and provide any required medical certification.

If the need for leave is not foreseeable, the employee must provide notification of leave to the employer as soon as is practicable under the circumstances. An employee's failure to provide thirty days' advance notification for foreseeable leave may result in a delay of leave.

Medical Certification

An employee who takes leave for the employee's serious health condition or to care for a family member with a serious health condition must submit to the nonprofit a medical certification of the need for such leave from the applicable health care provider. Failure to provide the certification promptly may result in a delay of leave.

The nonprofit may request a second or third medical opinion at the nonprofit's expense for verification of an employee's serious health condition. The opinion of the third health care provider, who is approved jointly by the nonprofit and the employee, shall be final and binding on the employer and the employee.

In addition, while the employee is on leave, the nonprofit may require the employee to provide periodic recertification of the employee's medical condition (not to exceed once every thirty days), and the employer may inquire as to the employee's intentions to return to work.

An employee on uninterrupted, continuous leave due to the employee's own serious health condition will be required to provide a job-related medical certification of fitness before being allowed to return to work. Failure to provide this certification may result in the delay or denial of job restoration.

Benefits Continuation

The same health care benefits coverage provided to an employee on the day before taking family and medical leave will be maintained during the twelve-week leave provided the employee continues to pay any required contribution for benefits. Employees who are on leave are responsible for making periodic payment of the required contribution to the nonprofit.

Upon completion of the twelve-week leave, or if an employee fails to maintain his or her contribution for benefits or fails to return to work at the end of the leave, a loss of coverage will occur and continuation of health care coverage would be offered through COBRA. An employee who does not return from leave may be required, under certain circumstances provided by the Family Medical and Leave Act, to reimburse the nonprofit for any employee contributions paid by the nonprofit while the employee was on unpaid leave.

While on leave, an employee must continue to pay the premiums or loan payments for any applicable benefits that would otherwise be automatically deducted from the employee's wages (e.g., supplemental life insurance, credit union loans, employee 401(k) savings plan loans). Contact the Internal Operations Department for details regarding employee premiums and/or loan payments.

The period of time an employee is on family and medical leave will be treated as continued service for purposes of vesting and eligibility to participate in any available pension or retirement plan. Absences due to leave will not be counted as time worked for the purpose of seniority or computing vacation, sick leave, or personal days.

Job Restoration

An employee will be returned to the same or an equivalent position when returning from family and medical leave, with no loss of benefits accrued before leave. An employee who does not return to work at the end of an authorized leave is subject to termination of employment.

In the event an employee's position with the nonprofit is affected by a decision or event not related to the employee's leave of absence (e.g., job elimination due to a reduction in force), the employee will be affected to the same extent as if not on leave.

Certain "key employees" as defined under the Family and Medical Leave Act of 1993 may not be eligible to be restored to the same or an equivalent position after leave if doing so would cause substantial and grievous economic injury to the operations of the assigned nonprofit. The nonprofit will notify such employees of their "key employee" status and the conditions under which job restoration will be denied, if applicable.

Questions about Family and Medical Leave

If you have any questions about your rights or responsibilities under this policy, contact the Internal Operations Department. The nonprofit will comply with all applicable federal, state, and local laws in administering this policy.

702 Continuation of Benefits

It is the policy of the nonprofit to provide the following health care benefits to employees who are away from work. All active full-time employees covered by the benefit plan will be eligible to continue medical coverage for twelve weeks following the beginning of an authorized paid or unpaid leave of absence or a temporary layoff due to lack of work.

An employee who is away from work for one of the above-stated reasons must pay the employee's share of employee coverage, including dependent coverage, if any, to maintain health care coverage during the time away from work.

Upon the expiration of twelve weeks, or if an employee fails to pay the employee contribution for benefits within thirty days from the established due date communicated to the employee and no applicable state or federal law provides otherwise, the employee's health care coverage, including dependent coverage, will be terminated. Continuation of health care coverage will be offered through COBRA.

703 Military Leaves of Absence

Leaves of absence without pay for military or reserve duty are granted to full-time regular and part-time regular employees. If an employee is called to active military duty or the reserve or National Guard training, or if the employee volunteers for the same, the employee should submit copies of military orders to the on-site supervisor as soon as possible.

Employees will be granted a military leave of absence without pay for the period of military service, in accordance with applicable federal and state laws.

If the employee is a reservist or a member of the National Guard, the employee is granted time off without pay for required military training. However, the employee may use any earned but unused vacation available. Eligibility for reinstatement after military duty or training is completed is determined in accordance with applicable federal and state laws.

704 Unpaid Personal Leave

In accordance with the guidelines set forth in this policy, the employer will consider providing unpaid personal leave to regular full-time employees who wish to take time off from work duties to fulfill personal obligations.

The unpaid personal leave may be granted for up to thirty calendar days every two years. If this initial period of absence proves insufficient, consideration will be given to a written request for a single extension of no more than thirty days. Pending the supervisor's approval, employees will take any available sick leave or vacation leave before the effective date of the personal leave of absence.

Requests for personal leave will be evaluated based on a number of factors, including anticipated operational requirements and staffing considerations during the proposed period of absence. The employer will continue to provide insurance benefits for the employee for the first thirty calendar days after the personal leave begins. At that time, employees must pay the full cost of their insurance benefits. The employer will resume payment of the costs of these benefits when the employee returns to active employment.

Accrual of benefit calculations, such as vacation, sick leave, or holiday benefits, will be suspended during the leave and will resume upon return to active employment.

To the extent possible, employees returning from personal leave will be reinstated to their former positions or offered the first-available comparable positions for which they are qualified.

If an employee fails to report to work at the agreed-upon time after the expiration of an approved leave period, employment termination will occur (Section 405, Employment Termination).

705 Educational Leave

In accordance with the guidelines set forth in this policy, the employer may consider providing unpaid educational leave to eligible *full-time* employees who wish to take time off from work duties to pursue course work that is applicable to their job duties with the nonprofit.

Employees may request educational leave up to six months every seven years. Requests will be evaluated based on a number of factors, including anticipated operational requirements and staffing considerations during the proposed period of absence. The employer will continue to provide insurance benefits for the employee for the full term of the educational leave. Accrual of benefit calculations, such as vacation, sick leave, or holiday benefits, will be suspended during the leave and will resume upon return to active employment.

To the extent possible, employees returning from educational leave will be reinstated to their former positions or be offered the first-available comparable positions for which they are qualified. If an employee fails to report to work after the expiration of an approved leave period, the employee is subject to disciplinary action or termination.

Employee Conduct and Disciplinary Action

801 Absenteeism and Tardiness

The nonprofit is able to serve our members based upon our estimates of performance and our history of reliability. Therefore, the nonprofit expects all employees to assume diligent responsibility for their attendance and promptness. Continued dependability, quality, and pride of service are factors over which each individual employee has a great deal of influence.

If you are absent and cannot perform your duties on time, or if you produce substandard work, then we all pay the price by losing the confidence of the clients.

The work schedule is constructed around the maximum working hours and capabilities of the staff. It is extremely important that you be punctual in your arrival for work at the beginning of the workday or shift to which you are assigned. If you know that you will be absent or late arriving for work, notify your supervisor within one hour of your scheduled start time by calling our main number.

If an employee is absent for more than three consecutive workdays, a statement from a physician may be required before the employee will be permitted to return to work. In such instances, the nonprofit also reserves the right to require the employee to submit to an examination by a physician designated by the nonprofit at its discretion.

Unexcused or excessive absenteeism or tardiness is grounds for disciplinary action, up to and including termination. If an employee is absent for three or more days and fails to report absences properly, this will be considered a resignation of the employee's position and the employee will be terminated for abandonment of the job.

802 Guidelines for Appropriate Conduct

As a nonprofit team member, the employee is expected to accept certain responsibilities, follow acceptable principles in matters of conduct, and exhibit a high degree of integrity at all times. This not only involves sincere respect for the rights and feelings of others, but it also demands that employees refrain from any behavior that might be harmful to themselves, their coworkers, and the nonprofit, or that might be viewed unfavorably by current or potential clients or by the public at large. Employee conduct reflects on the nonprofit. Employees are, consequently, encouraged to observe the highest standards of professionalism at all times.

Types of behavior and conduct that the nonprofit considers inappropriate include, but are not limited to, the following:

◆ Falsifying employment or other nonprofit records

◆ Violating the nonprofit's nondiscrimination and/or sexual harassment policy

◆ Soliciting or accepting gratuities from clients

◆ Excessive absenteeism or tardiness

◆ Excessive, unnecessary, or unauthorized use of nonprofit property and supplies, particularly for personal purposes

◆ Reporting to work under the influence of drugs or alcohol, and the illegal manufacture, possession, use, sale, distribution, or transportation of drugs

◆ Bringing or using alcoholic beverages on the nonprofit property or using alcoholic beverages while engaged in nonprofit business off the nonprofit's premises

◆ Fighting or using obscene, abusive, or threatening language or gestures

◆ Theft of property from coworkers, clients, or the nonprofit

◆ Unauthorized possession of firearms on the nonprofit premises or while on nonprofit business

◆ Disregarding safety or security regulations

◆ Insubordination

◆ Failing to maintain the confidentiality of nonprofit, client, or client information

◆ Continually failing to meet the expectations of the employee's supervisor with respect to work performed, behavior, ability, and willingness to work productively with others

◆ Failure to maintain a neat, clean, and professional personal appearance

◆ Allowing work performance to be negatively impaired by your personal business

◆ Failure to respect employer and client confidentiality

◆ Failure to follow federal and state civil rights laws

◆ Failure to maintain appropriate and accurate documentation

Should your performance, work habits, overall attitude, conduct, or demeanor become unsatisfactory based on violations either of the above or of any other nonprofit policies, rules, or regulations, you will be subject to disciplinary action, up to and including termination. Before or during the imposition of any discipline, employees may be given an opportunity to relate their version of incidents or problems at issue and provide any explanation or justification they consider relevant.

Where appropriate, a policy of *Progressive Employee Discipline* will be followed by supervisors. Major responsibilities of this policy include:

◆ *Oral reprimand*—The first step in the nonprofit's progressive disciplinary policy is the "oral reprimand." This is an oral warning that an employee's conduct is unacceptable and that repeated or continued failure to conform conduct or performance to the nonprofit standards will result in more severe disciplinary action. Before receiving an oral reprimand, the employee will be counseled by a supervisor and told what improvements are necessary and expected to correct any performance deficiencies. A record of the notice of the oral reprimand may be made and retained in the employee's personnel file.

◆ *Written reprimand*—The second step is a "written reprimand." This reprimand will describe the unacceptable conduct or performance of the employee and specify needed changes or improvements. A copy of the written reprimand will be retained in the employee's personnel file.

◆ *Suspension*—Suspension of the employee's employment may, at the sole discretion of the nonprofit, be used as a third step. The length of the suspension will vary based on such factors as the severity of the offense, the employee's performance, and the employee's disciplinary record. An employee may be suspended for repeated instances of minor misconduct, failure to conform conduct or performance to the standards of the position, or a single serious offense. A record of the suspension will be retained in the employee's personnel file.

◆ *Termination*—The final step in the disciplinary procedure is the termination of the employee. If an employee fails to conform conduct or performance to the standards required by the nonprofit, the nonprofit may, in its sole discretion, terminate the employee's employment.

Notwithstanding the preceding progressive disciplinary procedure policy, the nonprofit reserves the right to administer discipline in such a manner as it deems appropriate to the circumstances and may, in its sole discretion, eliminate any or all the steps in the progressive discipline procedure.

803 Complaint-Resolution Procedures

Misunderstandings or conflicts can arise in any nonprofit. To ensure effective working relations, it is important that such matters be resolved before serious problems develop. Most incidents resolve themselves naturally; however, should a situation persist that you believe is detrimental to your employment with the nonprofit, you should follow the procedure described here for bringing your complaint to management's attention.

◆ *Step 1*. Discussion of the problem with your immediate supervisor is encouraged as a first step. If, however, you do not believe a discussion with your supervisor is appropriate, you may proceed directly to step two.

◆ *Step 2.* If your problem is not resolved after discussion with your supervisor or if you feel discussion with your supervisor is inappropriate, you are encouraged to request a meeting with a representative of the human resources department. In an effort to resolve the problem, the representative will consider the facts and may conduct an investigation.

The nonprofit does not tolerate any form of retaliation against employees availing themselves of this procedure. The procedure should not be construed, however, as preventing, limiting, or delaying the nonprofit from taking disciplinary action against any individual, up to and including termination, in circumstances (such as those involving problems of overall performance, conduct, attitude, or demeanor) where the nonprofit deems disciplinary action appropriate.

804 Antiharassment Policy

Policy Requiring Reporting of Any Harassment of Employees

The nonprofit is committed to providing a work environment that is free of harassment of all kinds while working. More specifically, it is the nonprofit's policy that none of its employees may be subjected to harassment of any kind, but particularly harassment forbidden by law such as harassment because of one's race, sex, ethnicity, age, religion, national origin, color, weight, height, marital status, veteran status, or disability. This prohibition includes, of course, sexual harassment as described in the policy against sexual harassment.

All types of harassment are prohibited, and the employer will take strong disciplinary steps, up to and including discharge, against any employee who engages in it.

It is also the policy of the employer that any employee who believes that he or she has been subjected to such harassment must report that fact immediately in writing to the executive director. The report will be promptly investigated and remedial action will be undertaken as appropriate. To the extent possible, the investigation will be conducted in a manner calculated to protect the privacy of the individuals involved. When a report of harassment is made in good faith, the employer will protect the employee from retaliation or any other detrimental impact on his or her employment.

Anti-Sexual-Harassment Policy

It is the policy of the nonprofit to maintain a working environment that encourages mutual respect, promotes respectful and congenial relationships between employees, and is free from all forms of harassment of any employee or applicant for employment by anyone, including supervisors, coworkers, vendors, or customers. Harassment in any manner or form is expressly prohibited and will not be tolerated by the nonprofit. Accordingly, nonprofit management is committed to vigorously enforcing this policy against harassment, including, but not limited to, sexual harassment, at all levels within the nonprofit.

All reported or suspected occurrences of harassment will be promptly and thoroughly investigated. Where harassment is determined to have occurred, the nonprofit will immediately take appropriate disciplinary action, including written warnings and possible suspension, transfer and/or termination. The nonprofit will not permit or condone any acts of retaliation against anyone who files harassment complaints or cooperates in the investigation of same.

The term "harassment" includes but is not limited to unwelcome slurs, jokes, verbal, graphic or physical conduct relating to an individual's race, religion, sex, age, national origin, or disability.

Sexual harassment consists of unwelcome sexual advances, requests for sexual favors, or other verbal or physical conduct of a sexual nature where:

◆ submission to such conduct is an explicit or implicit term or condition of employment;

◆ employment decisions are based on an employee's submission to or rejection of such conduct; or

◆ such conduct interferes with an individual's work performance or creates an intimidating, hostile or offensive working environment.

The term "harassment" may also include the conduct of employees, supervisors, vendors and/or customers who engage in verbally or physically harassing behavior which has the potential for humiliating or embarrassing an employee of the nonprofit.

Complaint Procedure

The nonprofit provides its employees with a convenient and reliable method for reporting incidents of harassment, including sexual harassment.

Any employee who feels that they have been or are being harassed, or discriminated against, is encouraged to immediately inform the alleged harasser that the behavior is unwelcome. In most instances, the person is unaware that their conduct is offensive and when so advised can easily and willingly correct the conduct so that it does not recur.

If the informal discussion with the alleged harasser is unsuccessful in remedying the problem or if such an approach is not possible, the employee should immediately report the complained-of conduct to their immediate supervisor, manager, executive director, or if preferable, to the human resources department. The report should include all facts available to the employee regarding the harassment.

Confidentiality

All reports of harassment will be treated seriously. However, absolute confidentiality is not promised nor can it be assured. The nonprofit will conduct an investigation of any complaint that will require limited disclosure of pertinent information to certain parties, including the alleged harasser.

Investigative Procedure

Once a complaint is received, the nonprofit will begin a prompt and thorough investigation. The investigation may include interviews with all involved employees, including the alleged harasser, and any employees who are aware of facts or incidents alleged to have occurred.

Once the investigation is completed, a determination will be made regarding the validity of the harassment allegations. If it is determined that harassment has occurred, prompt, remedial action will be taken. This may include some or all of the following steps:

◆ Restore any lost terms, conditions, or benefits of employment to the complaining employee.

◆ Discipline the harasser. This discipline can include written disciplinary warnings, transfer, demotion, suspension, and termination.

If the harassment is from a vendor or customer, the nonprofit will take appropriate action to stop the complained-of conduct.

[e] Duties of Employees and Supervisors

All employees of the nonprofit, both management and nonmanagement, are responsible for ensuring that a workplace free of harassment is maintained. Any employee may file a harassment complaint regarding incidents experienced personally or incidents observed in the workplace. The nonprofit strives to maintain a lawful, pleasant work environment where all employees are able to effectively perform their work without interference of any type, and requests the assistance of all employees in this effort.

All nonprofit supervisors and managers are expected to adhere to the nonprofit's antiharassment policy. Supervisors' evaluations will include assessments of their efforts in following and enforcing this policy.

All managers and supervisors are responsible for doing all they can to prevent and discourage harassment from occurring. If a complaint is raised, supervisors and managers are to act promptly to notify the human resources department of the complaint so that human resources may proceed with an investigation. If supervisors or managers fail to follow this policy, they will be disciplined. Such discipline may include termination.

805 Drug and Alcohol Use

The policy of the nonprofit is to maintain a drug-free workplace. The term "workplace" is defined as nonprofit property, any nonprofit-sponsored activity, or any other site for the performance of work for the nonprofit. The term "drug" includes alcoholic beverages and prescription drugs as well as illegal inhalants and illegal drugs. Activities prohibited by this policy shall be considered grounds for discipline, including, but not limited to, suspension or immediate termination of employment if the activities occur in the workplace as defined above.

Prohibited activities under this policy include the unauthorized use of drugs, as defined above, in the workplace, including distribution, possession, or use of a drug or controlled substance as defined in Schedules I through V of the Controlled Substances Act, 21 SCUSC Section 812, 21 FRCFR Section 1308, and the state and local law of the jurisdiction where the workplace is located, including, but not by way of limitation, marijuana, opiates (e.g., heroin, morphine), cocaine, phencyclidine, and amphetamines. However, the use of prescription drugs, when taken as directed by a duly licensed physician, shall not be a violation of this policy.

To implement this policy, the nonprofit shall establish a drug-free awareness program that should inform employees of the following:

- ◆ The dangers of drug abuse in the workplace

- ◆ The nonprofit's policy of maintaining a drug-free workplace

- ◆ Any available drug counseling, rehabilitation, and employee assistance programs

- ◆ The penalties that may be imposed upon employees for drug-abuse and policy violations

Information regarding the availability of treatment programs, if any, such as assistance provided by the nonprofit's health care plan coverage, drug- and alcohol-abuse rehabilitation programs, and the requirements for participation in drug and alcohol abuse education and training programs, may be requested by contacting the human resources department.

All nonprofit employees shall be provided a copy of this policy and shall sign an acknowledgment of receipt of the policy and acceptance of its terms. As a condition of employment, all nonprofit employees must comply with this policy.

Any nonprofit employee who has been convicted under any criminal drug statute for a violation occurring in the workplace must report that conviction to the nonprofit no later than five days after the conviction. Within thirty days after receiving notice of the conviction described in this policy, the nonprofit shall impose discipline on, or require satisfactory participation in, a drug-abuse assistance or rehabilitation program by any employee who is convicted of a violation of a criminal drug statute if the violation occurred in the workplace.

This policy is not intended to replace or otherwise alter the obligation of the nonprofit to comply with requirements of the US Department of Transportation or any other federal, state, or local nonprofit that regulates drug-testing internal operations or a particular industry.

806 Firearms

(Note: In some states, laws allow for licensed gun owners to have guns in their vehicles. Check with your state on this issue.)

It is the intent of the nonprofit to provide a safe and secure workplace for employees, clients, customers of clients, visitors, and others with whom we do business. The nonprofit expressly forbids the possession of firearms on nonprofit property.

The nonprofit has a "zero tolerance" guideline for possession of any type of weapon, firearm, explosive, or ammunition. Nonprofit property includes, but is not limited to, all nonprofit facilities, vehicles, and equipment, whether leased or owned by the nonprofit or its client. In addition, firearms in employee-owned vehicles parked on nonprofit property are strictly forbidden.

The possession of firearms on nonprofit property may be cause for discipline, including immediate termination of employment. In enforcing this guideline, the nonprofit reserves the right to request inspections of any employee and the employee's personal effects, including personal vehicles, while on nonprofit premises. Any employee who refuses to allow inspection will be subject to the same disciplinary action as an employee found in possession of firearms.

Employees within the nonprofit share the responsibility of identifying violators of this guideline. An employee who witnesses or suspects another individual of violating this guideline should immediately report this information to the on-site supervisor.

807 Americans with Disabilities Act

The nonprofit supports the requirements of the Americans with Disabilities Act and state laws governing employment of individuals with disabilities. If you are such an individual, please advise management of your disability and the nature of accommodation necessary to enable you to perform the essential tasks of the job. If accommodation of your disability is feasible and does not create an undue hardship in the nonprofit's operations, we will work with you to find mutually agreeable solutions.

808 No-Smoking Policy

Smoking is prohibited on nonprofit property at all times. The nonprofit has implemented this program to protect individuals and provide a smoke-free working environment that is safe and healthy for staff, volunteers, and guests.

809 Solicitation and Distribution of Literature

It is the intent of the nonprofit to maintain a proper business environment and prevent interference with work and inconvenience to others from solicitations and/or distribution of literature other than that generated and approved by the nonprofit.

Group meetings for solicitation purposes, distributing literature, and circulating petitions during work hours or in work areas at any time is prohibited unless it is approved by the on-site supervisor as a nonprofit-sponsored event. The following guidelines will apply throughout the nonprofit:

◆ Employees will not engage in any solicitation of other employees for any purpose whatsoever during working hours or in work areas.

◆ The nonprofit's facilities may not be used as a meeting place that involves solicitation and/or distribution of literature.

◆ To maintain good customer relations and preserve the professional work environment, employees may not wear any insignias, badges, or buttons on themselves, or display any insignias, badges, or buttons on their desks or in their work areas, excluding professional designation awards.

◆ Certain types of information may be posted on the nonprofit's bulletin board. The human resources department will approve and post all information that is displayed on the nonprofit's bulletin board or make available for review or distribution to employees.

◆ Trespassing, soliciting, or distributing literature by anyone outside the nonprofit is prohibited on nonprofit premises.

810 Resignation Procedures

Resignation is a voluntary act initiated by the employee to terminate employment with the employer. Although advance notice is not required, the employer requests at least two weeks' written notice from all employees. Upon leaving, employees will be paid at their prevailing rate for accrued but unused vacation time. Vacation and sick leave time used but not yet accrued will be deducted from the employee's final pay.

Nonprofit

901 Nonprofit Assets

All assets and materials will be acquired and maintained in the nonprofit's name. Disposition of assets remains under the authority of the executive director or designated representative. All acquisitions are subject to budgetary constraints and are ultimately the responsibility of the senior executive director. Each division is responsible for identifying the level of its program needs.

902 Nonprofit Properties

The nonprofit provides equipment and tools to employees to use on the job. The tools and equipment remain the property of the nonprofit and are not to be used for personal projects. Each employee is responsible for the loss or damage of property due to the employee's negligence. All property provided to the employee must be returned to the nonprofit in the same condition as when it was received. If employment with the nonprofit terminates, the employee must return all property at the time of termination.

903 Business Expense Reimbursements

Staff traveling on the nonprofit's business will be reimbursed for approved business expenses incurred. Normal/approved travel is affirmed through regular communication with supervisors and development of division/position work plans.

Appropriate original documentation/receipts are required for all expense reimbursements. Documentation is the responsibility of the employee submitting the reimbursement request.

Employees required to use personal automobiles to fulfill job duties must have valid driver's licenses and be insured drivers of their vehicles and must maintain liability insurance coverage at levels at least equal to state law requirements. Employees will be reimbursed for mileage based on the IRS guidelines.

The nonprofit will maintain an IRS-recognized accountable reimbursement plan for employee business expense.

Appendix G—Employee Performance Plan

Description of Basic Responsibilities

The Employee Performance Plan is used by the employee and the supervisor to assist in the development of work objectives and in the review of past accomplishments. The plan provides the employee with both a general direction and specific work assignments to be completed in the coming year. The plan has three basic responsibilities: job objectives, performance review, and progress report.

Job Objectives

Normally, the job objectives will be set as part of the annual performance review, which should occur near the anniversary date of the hiring of the employee.

Purpose

The setting of job objectives is designed to provide employees and the supervisor with a system that does the following:

◆ Establishes a clear understanding of what is expected in the performance of a job

◆ Provides a basis for ongoing performance counseling and appraisal

◆ Forms a basis for planning future work activities

Definition

Objectives are work requirements, special projects, or activities assigned based on the job description, work plan, or special assignments. A written objective states what is to be accomplished, sets a time frame for the project, and sets a priority for it.

Examples

As much as possible, objectives should be specific, measurable, and stated in the following way: "to (action verb) a (specific results) by (specific date)." Specific action plans showing how the employee plans to achieve the objectives should also be included. Following are samples of objectives:

◆ To organize all personnel files and verify contents by October 15

◆ To organize department operations to achieve the following by October 15:

> ❖ Computerize client and volunteer information.

> ❖ Provide training to the staff on new computer systems.

◆ To develop and present to the board volunteer development policies/procedures by October 15

Steps for Setting Objectives

◆ At least two weeks before the annual performance review, the employee should make a list of obtainable objectives for the coming year.

◆ During the performance review, discuss the objectives with the supervisor and make any necessary changes and set priorities, completion dates, and review dates.

◆ Submit revised, final job objectives to the supervisor within two weeks after the performance review.

◆ At the semiannual progress report meeting with the supervisor, the job objectives should be reevaluated and adjustments made as needed.

Performance Review

Purpose

The primary purpose of the annual performance review is to do the following:

◆ Improve employee and supervisor communications so that the employee knows what is expected and how well expectations are being met.

◆ Assist staff in increasing competence in current positions, through fair and honest appraisals that identify areas for improvement as well as areas of strength.

◆ Provide a basis for a salary review.

◆ Provide an opportunity for employees to discuss career interests and plans for the future.

Guidelines

◆ Ongoing informal contacts and conferences during the year should provide for discussion of progress and accomplishments as well as problem areas.

◆ Regular communications will establish a realistic basis for the annual performance review.

◆ Mutual understanding of key job responsibilities and performance standards is assumed to have been reached before formal performance review.

◆ Evaluation comments must be based on representative information, not on isolated or unusual incidents. Suggested areas for improvement should be directed at actual work performance.

Steps for Performance Review

◆ Review by the employee and the supervisor of the job description, job objectives, and performance standards

◆ Discussion with the employee, by the supervisor, of the completed performance review

◆ Written comments by both the employee and the supervisor on the performance review signed by both and placed in the employee's personnel file

◆ Revised job objectives submitted by employee within two weeks of the performance review meeting, with a copy put into the employee's personnel file

◆ Any applicable comments from the semiannual progress report included in the performance review discussion

Criteria for Performance Review Ratings

◆ *Performed exceedingly well*: Accomplishments consistently exceed normal expected levels; makes significant contributions to work unit; rarely needs assistance; demonstrates creativity in problem solving; achievements clearly apparent.

◆ *Performed beyond requirements*: Accomplishments generally exceed expected work levels; meets all objectives and goals; gives extra effort and requires minimum supervision.

◆ *Performance meets requirements*: Accomplishments generally meet the expected level of work; steady, dependable performance; solid, dependable, conscientious employee.

◆ *Performance needs improvement*: Accomplishments generally below expected levels; unwilling or unable to meet work expectations; efforts are minimally acceptable at best; further counseling, training, and experience necessary to raise performance level.

◆ *Performance does not meet requirements*: Does not meet expected level of performance; unwilling or unable to meet expectations; work unacceptable.

Progressive Discipline Procedures

Should an employee have specific performance problems, progressive discipline procedures will be followed as outlined in the personnel policies (802 and 803).

Progress Report

Purpose: At least semiannually, the employee and the supervisor will review the job objectives and general job performance as finalized at the performance review.

Steps: Before the meeting, the employee and supervisor will complete a Progress Report form, adding recommendations for adjustments in performance and/or objectives, with a copy filed in the employee's personnel file.

Note: Some states are "hire and fire at will" states, meaning any employee may be dismissed with or without cause. (Check your state's laws on this issue.)

Acknowledgment of the Handbook

I acknowledge that I have received the nonprofit's Employee Handbook (the Handbook), dated _____, and understand that violations of the policies contained in the Handbook could result in disciplinary action, up to and including termination.

I further understand that the information contained in the Handbook represents guidelines for the nonprofit and that the nonprofit reserves the right to modify the Handbook or amend or terminate any policy, procedures, or employee benefit programs at any time.

I further understand that the contents of the Handbook do not form a written employment contract. Either the nonprofit or I have the right to terminate my employment at any time.

I further understand that no manager, supervisor, or representative of the nonprofit, other than the executive director, has any authority to enter into any agreement guaranteeing employment for any specific period of time. I also understand that any such agreement, if made, will not be enforceable unless it is in writing and signed by both parties.

I further understand that if I have any questions about the interpretation or application of any policies contained in the Handbook, I should direct these questions to the on-site supervisor.

_____   _____

Employee Signature   Date

_____

Name Printed

Social Security Number:_____

Witness Signature: _____

Please keep a copy of this acknowledgment for your records, and return the signed copy to your supervisor, which will be filed in your personnel file.

Appendix H—Types of Insurance

Unless the items marked with an asterisk (*) are specified in the policy as having higher or separate limits, claim payment for losses under them will be extremely limited.

Employee Benefits

◆ Unlimited major medical

◆ Disability to retirement age: short and long term, accident, and sickness

◆ Life insurance

◆ Pension or 401(k) plan

◆ Liability Insurance

General Liability

◆ Premises and operations

◆ Comprehensive

◆ Completed operations and products

◆ Contractual

◆ Personal injury

◆ Joint venture and liquor exclusion. *Host liquor liability should be included specifically if you ever serve alcoholic beverages, and coverage for joint ventures entered into after the policy date should be included automatically, with notice to the insurer.*

◆ Employees and volunteers defined as insured

◆ Notice of loss amended

◆ Employee and volunteer bonding

◆ Sexual misconduct, including sexual harassment

Professional Liability, Including Volunteers

Check on your state's "Good Samaritan" laws.

Insurance against Identity Theft and Hacker Prevention (Cybersecurity)

Fiduciary Liability

Directors and Officers Liability, with Employment Practices Liability

Umbrella

Including sexual misconduct, punitive damages not excluded, and the definition of who an insured is must be consistent with the wording of the underlying policy.

Property Insurance

- ◆ Perils covered
- ◆ Valuation of property
- ◆ Adequacy of limits
- ◆ Property of others
- ◆ Systems protection*
- ◆ Property in transit*
- ◆ Computer equipment*

Time Insurance

- ◆ Extra expense
- ◆ Leasehold interest

Crime Coverage

- ◆ Dishonesty
- ◆ Kidnap and ransom
- ◆ Forgery

Automobile Coverage

Including hired and nonowned coverage for volunteers; otherwise, volunteers driving their own vehicles while working for the agency would not be covered.

Workers' Compensation

Including coverage for volunteers if available in your state.

Index

CPSIA information can be obtained
at www.ICGtesting.com
Printed in the USA
FSOW03n1327120117
29513FS